M000231488

HUNTING THE ESSEX

THE HUNT FOR THE *ESSEX*

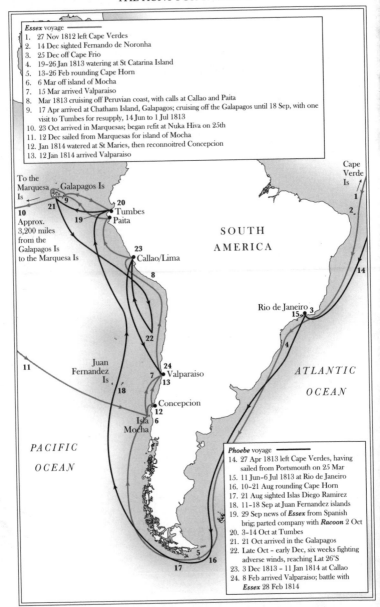

Essex voyage ———
1. 27 Nov 1812 left Cape Verdes
2. 14 Dec sighted Fernando de Noronha
3. 25 Dec off Cape Frio
4. 19–26 Jan 1813 watering at St Catarina Island
5. 13–26 Feb rounding Cape Horn
6. 6 Mar off island of Mocha
7. 15 Mar arrived Valparaiso
8. Mar 1813 cruising off Peruvian coast, with calls at Callao and Paita
9. 17 Apr arrived at Chatham Island, Galapagos; cruising off the Galapagos until 18 Sep, with one visit to Tumbes for resupply, 14 Jun to 1 Jul 1813
10. 23 Oct arrived in Marquesas; began refit at Nuka Hiva on 25th
11. 12 Dec sailed from Marquesas for island of Mocha
12. Jan 1814 watered at St Maries, then reconnoitred Concepcion
13. 12 Jan 1814 arrived Valparaiso

Cape Verde Is

SOUTH AMERICA

To the Marquesa Is
Galapagos Is
Approx. 3,200 miles from the Galapagos Is to the Marquesa Is

Tumbes
Paita

Callao/Lima

Rio de Janeiro

Juan Fernandez Is

Valparaiso

Concepcion

Isla Mocha

ATLANTIC OCEAN

PACIFIC OCEAN

Phoebe voyage ———
14. 27 Apr 1813 left Cape Verdes, having sailed from Portsmouth on 25 Mar
15. 11 Jun–6 Jul 1813 at Rio de Janeiro
16. 10–21 Aug rounding Cape Horn
17. 21 Aug sighted Islas Diego Ramirez
18. 11–18 Sep at Juan Fernandez islands
19. 29 Sep news of *Essex* from Spanish brig; parted company with *Racoon* 2 Oct
20. 3–14 Oct at Tumbes
21. 21 Oct arrived in the Galapagos
22. Late Oct – early Dec, six weeks fighting adverse winds, reaching Lat 26°S
23. 3 Dec 1813 – 11 Jan 1814 at Callao
24. 8 Feb arrived Valparaiso; battle with *Essex* 28 Feb 1814

Note that the numbered way-points are accurate, but the ships' tracks are approximate

HUNTING THE ESSEX

A Journal of the voyage of
HMS *Phoebe* 1813-1814

By Midshipman Allen Francis Gardiner

Edited by John S Rieske
Introduction by Professor Andrew Lambert

Seaforth
PUBLISHING

Transcription & notes © Estate of John S Rieske 2013
Introduction © Andrew Lambert 2013

First published in Great Britain in 2013 by
Seaforth Publishing
An imprint of Pen & Sword Books Ltd
47 Church Street, Barnsley
S Yorkshire S70 2AS

www.seaforthpublishing.com
Email info@seaforthpublishing.com

British Library Cataloguing in Publication Data
A CIP data record for this book is available
from the British Library

ISBN 978-1-84832-174-8

Typeset and designed by M.A.T.S, Leigh-on-Sea, Essex
Printed and bound in Great Britain
by CPI Group (UK) Ltd, Croydon, CR0 4YY

Contents

Editor's Preface   vi

A Note on Transcription   vii

Introduction by Professor Andrew Lambert   1

List of Illustrations   29

A Journal of the Proceedings of
H.M.S. *Phoebe* during a voyage to the
South Seas commencing March 25 1813
by Allen Francis Gardiner   32

Appendix: Related Documents   136

Notes   141

Bibliography   150

Editor's Preface

ASIDE FROM THE participants of the events here described, the fruition of this book should be attributed years ago to an almost discarded, unbound copy of Volume I of the second edition of Captain David Porter's book, *Journal of a Cruise Made to the Pacific Ocean, by Captain David Porter, in the United States Frigate Essex in the Years 1812, 1813, and 1814*, published in 1822. This portion of a book I found in a small shop selling used books and acquired it for the sum of a few dollars, then considered adequate. I read this book avidly, entranced by the rollicking adventures of the ship's captain and crew, during their pauses at the Galapagos and Marquesas Islands in the Pacific Ocean. Only after acquiring a copy of the first edition printed in 1815 did I learn the details of the naval battle between the USS *Essex* and the British frigate HMS *Phoebe* commanded by Captain James Hillyar, occurring on 28 March 1814 off the port of Valparaiso, Chile. This account was lacking in Volume I of the two-volume 1822 edition.

Porter's account of the cruise of the *Essex* was published in four editions, two in the United States, 1815 and 1822, Italy, 1820, and Great Britain, 1823 as well as in a number of historical reviews including a biography of David Porter by his son Admiral David Dixon Porter. At least two novels directly based on this voyage have also been published, while Patrick O'Brian's *Far Side of the World* (1984) was loosely inspired by its events, with the part of the *Essex* played by a fictitious USS *Norfolk*. This in turn provided the basis for Peter Weir's film *Master & Commander*, where the frigate was transformed into a

French privateer, although one built in America. Ironically, there is a dearth of contemporaneous publications about the victorious British part in this historic epic – John C Fredriksen's annotated bibliography *War of 1812 Eyewitness Accounts* (Westport 1997) lists nothing more than Hillyar's official dispatch.

Thus, when the manuscript journal written by Allen Francis Gardiner, a junior officer aboard the *Phoebe* during its search for the *Essex* and its attack on the *Essex* appeared at auction, I was determined to obtain it if possible. The term 'if possible' expresses a real sticking point because the auction was to be held near the coast of Massachusetts, an area wedded to the ocean and the vessels and men sailing on it. After driving 500 miles and staying a night at a Bed and Breakfast I was surprised that I was able to obtain the desired manuscript journal with an affordable bid. I don't know if I was bidding against a dealer in rare marine publications who had his business in the area, and would have been aware of the true value of the journal. But fortune smiled on me! So I hope that this book will fill a void in the history of the encounter between the *Essex* and the *Phoebe*.

Of additional value in Gardiner's journal is the extensive description and commentary by a twenty-year old officer of the geography and social interactions in the ports of call in Spanish South America during the early nineteenth century. He found particularly abhorrent the popular but brutal sport of bullfighting. This sensitivity to the cruel treatment of animals may appear inconsistent with the harsh discipline that he must have observed during his naval service, where to modern eyes punishments often amounted to torture. However, discipline aboard a ship at sea during long voyages with privation and boredom is necessary for survival, in contrast to gratuitous torture of an animal for entertainment only.

Understandably, as a dashing young naval officer, he was a connoisseur of the attractions of the fairer sex in these ports and of the food and drink served on banquet tables. However, for the general reader one slight surprise of the journal is that Gardiner reveals very little about life in the British Navy, but this is undoubtedly because he aimed his work at other service people who would be familiar already with the everyday workings of the Navy.

John S Rieske, PhD,
Professor Emeritus, The Ohio State University.
Columbus, Ohio, USA

A Note on Transcription

Gardiner's narrative was transcribed from his original handwritten journal, and the text of the manuscript is reproduced as near as possible to the way it was written in order to retain a sense of authenticity. In a few minor cases deliberate alterations have been made to grammar, spelling, or punctuation to clarify ambiguity, but some uncertainties remain due to Gardiner's penmanship, which renders many letters of the alphabet, particularly the vowels, indistinguishable from each other; nor was it always easy to identify intentional punctuation from spots, blots and other extraneous marks. Furthermore, for a small number of unfamiliar terms, names, and places the transcriptions were essentially educated guesses, particularly in the case of his poetry where the context does not make the meaning obvious.

Introduction

THE SOUTH PACIFIC cruise of the American frigate USS
Essex during the War of 1812, her successful raid on the
British whaling fleet and the dramatic final battle that led
to her capture at Valparaiso has been a classic tale of the
sea for two hundred years. The voyage achieved legendary
status in the United States, largely through the publication
of Captain David Porter's narrative account. In the absence
of an alternative, British, perspective on those events,
Porter's story, which has been repeated by most subsequent
authors, has dominated the literature.[1] In truth Porter's
book did far more than recount his experiences; it created
an American South Pacific, an ocean occupied by whaling
ships and dotted with tropical islands, many of them
populated by primitive peoples with remarkable customs
and sexual mores.

While Allen Francis Gardiner's journal lacks the scale
and significance of Porter's book – he had nothing to
excuse or explain – it does provide a contrasting British
perspective on an important episode, and a bloody battle.
Gardiner compiled his journal while serving on board
HMS *Phoebe*, the British frigate that hunted down and
captured the *Essex*. Not only does Gardiner's account add
depth and shade to the story, challenging key aspects of
Porter's account in the process, but it also opens a wider
perspective on the South Pacific in the age of revolution.
Phoebe rounded Cape Horn, visited the romantic islands
of Juan Fernandez, which turned out to be a prison camp,
the Galapagos before Darwin, the mainland ports of

Guayaquil, Tumbes, Callao and Valparaiso. Gardiner also visited Lima, the capital of Spanish Peru. His journal is packed with telling details of the famous American ship, her crew and the action in which she was taken. Behind the written texts lies a deep well of unspoken assumptions, the mental world of contemporary naval officers, revealed in words left unwritten, and the ideas that underpin those that were.

The Author

Allen Francis Gardiner was born on 28 January 1794, the youngest son of an Oxfordshire gentleman. After a religious education he entered the Royal Naval College at Portsmouth in May 1808, where he mastered the techniques and tools of his profession before joining his first ship two years later. After a brief period serving in the Mediterranean Gardiner joined HMS *Phoebe*, Captain James Hillyar, in time to take part in a successful squadron action with three French frigates off the coast of Madagascar on 20 May 1811, in which seven men were killed and twenty-four wounded taking the frigate *Renommeé*. By an irony of fate that would not have been lost on Gardiner, this ship would be taken and burnt by the USS *Constitution* off the coast of Brazil on 29 December 1812, while serving her new owners as HMS *Java*. When, as Samuel Thornton reported, the crew of the USS *Essex* threatened to give the *Phoebe* 'Java's time for it' they had no idea that the *Phoebe* had taken the *Java*.[2] Six days later a second French frigate was taken, along with the tiny French fort at Tamatave. The following year *Phoebe* took part in the capture of the Dutch colony of Java before returning to England.

As befits a young man of his background and education Gardiner brought a cultured mind to his task, conditioned by the markedly evangelical tone that informed his judgement of foreign cities, peoples and customs. Modern readers share his condemnation of slavery, and his revulsion at the sustained carnage of the Lima bullring, but his analysis of South American peoples reflected contemporary assumptions of racial and cultural superiority. In his eyes any people who exploited slaves and took their entertainment from sustained animal cruelty were inferior. Gardiner combined the scientific curiosity of a newly minted trainee naval officer with the aesthetic sensibilities of a young man trained to paint coastal perspectives and write accurate reports to improve navigational knowledge, and a taste for fine writing cultivated by reading and writing poetry. Gardiner's text is complemented by the suitably upbeat report of the voyage and the battle that Midshipman Samuel Thornton sent to his father on 12 April 1814. Born in 1797 Thornton was three years younger than Gardiner, but had been at sea since 1811. His father was a City merchant, a Director of the Bank of England and an MP, which may explain how he came to start his career on board the frigate HMS *Amazon,* under her renowned Captain William Parker.[3] He transferred to the *Phoebe* when Parker's ship paid off, to serve under another great frigate commander, Captain James Hillyar.

The War of 1812
While the War of 1812 was dominated by the American overland invasion of modern Canada and attacks on British shipping in the North Atlantic and Caribbean, oceanic warfare eventually stretched across the globe.[4] In

the six moths that followed the outbreak of war in June 1812 American warships and privateers reaped a rich harvest of British merchant ships. This windfall was short-lived; by the end of the year the Royal Navy was able to establish an effective convoy system and began to blockade the key American ports of Boston, New York, Baltimore, Charleston and Savannah. Once the British took control of the Atlantic, American ships were forced to look ever further afield for prizes: the sheer ubiquity of British commerce meant that all the world's oceans were filled with British merchant vessels. In 1813 the frigate USS *President* set off for the Arctic, where she joined forces with two American privateers. Other American officers and strategists planned to enter Asian waters, the Indian Ocean routes of the East India Company, the greatest of all trading conglomerates, and the high profile China trade. Large ships laden with silks, porcelain, tea, silver and opium, made attractive targets. Confident that they would find British defences in these waters weak or non-existent, the Americans looked for rich rewards, while diverting British attention away from their own coast. These plans reflected deep-rooted American desires to challenge the British in Asia.

While the route to China via the Indian Ocean was relatively well-known to American seafarers, the South Pacific remained a sea of dreams – a vast empty space seemingly purpose-made to take the imprint of an American vision. Pre-war whaling and fur trade expeditions held out the promise of limitless catches and massive profits. President Thomas Jefferson (1800-1808) had sent an overland expedition to the Pacific North West, as part of his plan to control the continent, while New England seafarers sought commercial profits trading furs into the Chinese market. Twenty years' experience of Asian trade influenced American wartime strategy. Not only did naval officers consider the China Seas, Indian and Pacific Oceans highly attractive, but Navy Secretary William Jones, in office 1813-14, possessed extensive experience in Asian trade. This experience dominated his strategy.[5] However, the British had two centuries of experience defending trade in distant waters, and detailed knowledge of American navigation in Indian and Chinese waters.[6] Any move the Americans made would meet a swift and effective response.

Astoria and the Fur Trade Empire

North West Coast sea otter pelts had been the most profitable American export to China before the War, prompting John Jacob Astor to found the modestly named trade post of Astoria in 1811.[7] Astor's dream of sustaining windfall profits in China depended on official support. After the outbreak of war President James Madison and Treasury Secretary Albert Gallatin made fur trade expansion part of national strategy. They had little choice: the administration desperately needed Astor's financial support. During the war Astor loaned a penniless government $2.5 million, in return for worthless promises to defend his Pacific trade post.[8] In the event the American Government did nothing, earning Astor's undying contempt. Astor's British competitors, the North West Company, also secured Government support. They sent two forces to seize Astoria. The armed store ship *Isaac Todd* left Portsmouth on 25 March 1813, escorted by the frigate HMS *Phoebe*. Captain James Hillyar had orders to 'totally annihilate any settlement which the Americans may have formed either on the Columbia River or on the neighbouring coast.' He would rendezvous with a second force, 100 men who travelled overland to the American post. As this expedition was heading into relatively unknown waters the Admiralty encouraged him to secure ethnographic and hydrographic intelligence.[9] These scientific subjects featured in the official reports, and in Gardiner's journal. In October 1813 the North West Company overland expedition reached Astoria with news of war. Astor's agents preferred business to violence, selling the post and the furs for $58,000, a fair market value, on the 16th. The deal done the Americans left. Astor was furious: he had lost a lot of money, and far worse, a business opportunity. Long before news of this success could reach London the North West Company's plans collided with the wider War of 1812 when an American naval officer began an unauthorised raid into the Pacific.

Captain David Porter, the USS *Essex* and the Pacific
Before the war Captain David Porter USN (1780-1843) had proposed a Pacific voyage of exploration and colonisation to the Navy Secretary. Although nothing came of his plans the war provided an opportunity to put them into practice. Sent to join Commodore William Bainbridge's three-ship squadron in October 1812, Porter, commanding the frigate USS *Essex*, never met the *Constitution* and the *Hornet*. Finding no sign of Bainbridge at Porto Praya in the Cape Verde Islands or on the Brazilian coast Porter captured the Post Office Packet *Nocton* on 12 December, which yielded £15,000 in specie.[10] He took another British ship off Rio de Janeiro

at the end of December, before deciding that his discretionary orders to act 'for the good of the service' would cover a voyage round Cape Horn.[11] His pre-war project provided ample information about the trade and shipping of the South Pacific. He knew that several Spanish South American colonies were in revolt, and might provide a sympathetic welcome to an American republican warship.[12] His target would be the British Pacific whaling industry; the whale ships were well-equipped and richly laden, while there were no British warships in the Pacific.[13]

After a stormy passage round Cape Horn *Essex* received a warm welcome at the Chilean port of Valparaiso on 15 March 1813. The revolutionary regime provided food, water and naval stores, and after an eight-day refit Porter headed out to sea. Cruising off the Galapagos Islands between the 29 April and 18 September he took twelve largely unsuspecting British whalers. Porter fitted two as auxiliary raiders, and released the two oldest ships to their captains to carry prisoners to Rio. Later Porter would claim to have inflicted $5 million in damage, over £1 million at the contemporary exchange rate, on the British. In fact most prizes were recaptured, and only one actually reached the United States, as a prisoner exchange cartel.

In September Porter took the *Essex* to the little known Marquesas Islands to refit. Arriving at Nuka Hiva on 25 October he warped the *Essex* into the bay and began a major overhaul of the ship and her rigging. Between the refit and waging war on a recalcitrant local tribe Porter annexed the island to the United States.[14] His brief Pacific empire collapsed soon after he left. Having refitted *Essex* and prepared to send his prizes home Porter gave way to the overriding obsession of American frigate captains, a desperate desire for personal glory in single combat. He sailed back to Valparaiso, fully expecting to encounter Captain James Hillyar and HMS *Phoebe*. Gripped by this fixation Porter ignored the fact that his pursuit of personal glory was entirely at odds with his orders, and American national interests. The *Essex* reached Valparaiso, with the armed prize *Essex Junior* in company on 12 January. In his absence the political scene had changed: the friends of March 1813 had fallen from power, their successors, fearing a Spanish counter-attack, put their faith in the overwhelming power of the Royal Navy.[15]

Pursuing Porter

News of Porter's initial arrival at Valparaiso reached Buenos Aires in May 1813. Captain Peter Heywood, once of HMS *Bounty*, forwarded a letter from British merchants reporting the enthusiastic reception given to the *Essex*, and reports that Porter had 'gone out to take and destroy the English whalers on the coast'.[16] This news was soon in the hands of Admiral Manley Dixon commanding the Brazils station from Rio de Janeiro. The Royal Navy's effective global intelligence network ensured a swift response to Porter's Pacific cruise. When the news reached him in June 1813 Dixon had already secured the main Atlantic trade routes, before turning his attention to the Pacific. At the same time the North West Company expedition arrived at Rio. When the North West Company officers revealed the details of the mission Dixon consulted Hillyar, detaching the ship sloops *Cherub* and *Racoon* to guard the whale fishery while the *Phoebe* went to Astoria.[17] He placed the smaller ships under Hillyar's command; he had planned to send another frigate to pursue the *Essex*, but resources failed him. Suitably reinforced Hillyar should be able to deal with the *Essex*, escort the *Isaac Todd*, and re-open trade with Peru.[18] In view of the immense distances involved he gave Hillyar complete discretion, subject to the direction that he must remain strictly neutral between the Spanish imperial regime in Lima and the revolted colonies.[19]

The newly independent Chilean government had opened its ports to British traders in 1811, creating valuable opportunities just as Napoleon's Continental System threatened to undermine the economic basis of British power. However, the trade remained risky, the Spanish authorities in Peru seizing British ships. The value of British commerce to local merchants and the long naval arm of the British state meant that when Porter tried to sell some of his prizes at Valparaiso British protests blocked any sales. The turn of the tide of war at sea helped restore British prestige. The 'glorious' news that HMS *Shannon* had captured the USS *Chesapeake* made 'all Englishmen hold their heads very high, and the Americans lower their tone considerably'. Heywood reported American influence at Buenos Aires was 'much on the decline'. The distant resonance of Philip Broke's brilliant action emphasised the remarkable resilience of British power.

After leaving Rio on 6 July Hillyar set a series of rendezvous for wood and water that avoided contact with the South American mainland, including Juan Fernandez and the Galapagos Islands. While rounding Cape Horn the warships became separated from the sluggish *Isaac Todd*, to Gardiner's obvious delight. After an unexpectedly easy passage the original plan to make directly for Valparaiso was abandoned. Light winds made it necessary to seek refreshment at the romantic islands of Juan Fernandez. After watering Hillyar headed north. In mid-October, as he neared the equator, he picked up recent intelligence that suggested the *Isaac Todd* had been taken by the *Essex*. Detaching *Racoon* to the Columbia River he took *Cherub* in company and decided to search for the American ship.[20] *Racoon* reached the Columbia on 30 November 1813 to find the North West Company had already secured the fort, by commercial transaction.[21] Meanwhile Hillyar picked up Porter's trail, calling at Tumbes, Guayaquil, Callao and the Galapagos Islands.[22] English sailors liberated at Tumbes provided more intelligence about the elusive American, and useful advice on the offshore island groups.[23]

Finally, on 8 February *Phoebe* and *Cherub* sailed into Valparaiso Bay. Hillyar found the British commercial community anxious to help, offering intelligence on the American ship, local navigation and Chilean politics. The merchant ship *Emily* intercepted the inbound frigate and her master, one time naval officer George O'Brien, proved very useful, being well acquainted with the port. Porter had been expecting the British ships; he even knew their names. He planned a two-ship action, using his weaker consort to draw off the *Cherub,* while the *Essex* closed with *Phoebe* under a Spanish flag.[24] As he sailed into the harbour Hillyar tried to provoke a battle, on the advice of George O'Brien, who knew the Americans were short-handed, with many men ashore. To avoid violating Chilean neutrality Hillyar tried to goad the Americans to fire first. In the event most of the *Essex's* men had returned to the ship by the time Hillyar ranged alongside, and Porter held his fire. Porter claimed that *Phoebe* came very close; just as Hillyar enquired after his health the two ships almost collided. Despite being in neutral waters Porter threatened to engage, calling up his crew and hoisting kedge anchors to the ends of the yards to grapple the enemy. With *Essex* fully manned and ready for combat Hillyar wisely hauled off.[25] Both Gardiner and Thornton provide fresh insight into this incident.

The following day the two ships engaged in a boisterous display of nationalistic pride. *Essex* hoisted a large white flag marked 'Free Trade and Sailor's Rights' to the fore topgallant masthead, just like James Lawrence in the *Chesapeake*. To counter this 'insidious effort to shake the loyalty of thoughtless British Seamen' Hillyar returned the compliment with a rather wordy riposte, sewn onto an English Flag: 'God and Country, British Sailors Best Rights. Traitors Offend Both'. Then Hillyar played 'God Save the King', the crew manned the rigging and gave three rousing cheers.[26] Although Porter later paraded his men ashore with flags bearing well-worn American slogans Gardiner reported several British sailors left the *Essex*. The very public use of the word 'Traitor' reminded any British sailors among the *Essex's* crew that if they were captured the British would be looking for deserters.[27] Many knew the grim fate of the deserters on board the USS *Chesapeake* on 1 June 1813 – most were killed in battle, or threw themselves into the sea; only one survived to face a Court Martial and death by public hanging. Gardiner went on to stress that fear of capture led Porter's men to remain at their posts after the battle had been lost, and try to get ashore after the ship surrendered. There were a significant number of British sailors on board the *Essex,* and many of them had deserted from the Royal Navy.

Unable to fight in the neutral waters of Valparaiso harbour the two crews taunted each other with shouted insults, songs and flags, while the officers compiled wordy salutations impugning the honour, courage or morality of their potential opponents. The British example printed in the Appendix may have been composed by Gardiner, the only officer of the *Phoebe* at this time known to write poetry. While it is not a work of any literary merit, it is both well-informed and solidly constructed. The object is to humiliate the Americans by holding up their own actions to scrutiny and judgement. Verses 6 and 7 refer to the tarring and feathering of a British sailor by *Essex's* crew at the outbreak of War in 1812, while 4 and 5, 7 and 8 deal with Porter's occupation of the Marquesas Islands. The composition would have been enjoyed by the primary audience, fellow wardroom officers, who needed a little entertainment. No doubt the verses were declaimed after dinner, toasted and cheered before being copied out in a fine hand, and despatched to the *Essex*.[28]

Such tomfoolery aside, Hillyar had found his prey, and he had no intention of allowing Porter to escape. He held station off the harbour, watched and waited; the cat and mouse game favoured the calm and collected Hillyar over his impetuous opponent. The *Phoebe* was slightly larger than the *Essex* while her conventional armament – a gun deck battery of 26 long 18-pounders – gave Hillyar a massive advantage in long-range firepower over the 32-pounder carronade battery of the *Essex*, although at close quarters the odds would be reversed. Furthermore, *Phoebe* was a proven winner, and *Cherub* was vastly superior to

Porter's consort, the armed whaler *Essex Junior*.

While Porter waited the noose was tightening. By March 1814 two more British frigates were heading for the South Pacific. Finally Porter accepted that Hillyar would not waste his decisive advantage, and that more British ships would arrive before long. His sources confirmed that they were the 18-pounder frigates *Tagus* and *Briton,* both larger than his own ship. Once Hillyar had two frigates, let alone three, Porter could expect an attack. He had to escape, and soon. Hillyar knew this, maintaining a thorough watch with the help of British merchants based ashore.

Porter hoped to mislead his opponent, sending the ship's purser ashore to conduct further business on 27 March, making sure that this was reported to Hillyar. He hoped the British would lower their guard. On the night of 27-28 March Porter sent a boat out to sea, firing rockets and burning blue lights, hoping to draw *Phoebe* to leeward, clearing the way for *Essex* to escape at daybreak. Hillyar, as Gardiner reports, was not fooled. By dawn he had resumed station dead to windward of the *Essex's* anchorage, a serious test of his seamanship. Expecting action Hillyar, ever the attentive professional, set the patriotic watchword 'God Save the King' in case his men became mixed up with the Americans when boarding. Such things were unnecessary when the enemy spoke another language.[29]

At first light Hillyar could see the *Essex* at anchor. He may not have realised just how disappointed Porter was to see *Phoebe* and *Cherub* 'close to the weather point of the Bay'. He had expected them to be off to leeward, giving him a chance to escape. To remind the Americans that they were being closely watched by well-handled ships, Hillyar wore inside the point and then wore out again. In the afternoon the wind strengthened from the SSW and Porter having stowed all the *Essex's* ground tackle, cut his last cable, which belonged to a prize, and made a run for the sea. Hillyar responded immediately, closing to cut off his escape past the Point of Angels. Then *Essex* was hit by a heavy squall, which carried away the main topmast at the lower cap. The damage aloft ended any hope of escape, so Porter wore ship onto the starboard tack, cleared the wreckage and cut away the mainsail and main topsail, which were flying out of control. The sacrifice of canvas was essential; flapping sails would hamper his attempt to work back into Valparaiso Bay. Judging his crippled ship would be unable to fetch her old anchorage inside Point of Angels, Porter bore up for a small bay on the other side of the harbour, five to six miles from the town, and at least two miles from the nearest Chilean fort (the fort was not in sight of the ship). Hillyar saw the main topmast fall, and the sudden change of course. At 3.45 (4.00 on *Phoebe*) *Essex* dropped her spare anchor in the Bay, in 9½ fathoms of water about 25 yards from the shore. Porter had two ensigns aloft, on the fore and mizzen topmasts: 'Free Trade and Sailor's Rights' and 'God our Country and Liberty. Tyrants offend them'. Hillyar had plenty of time to note the mottos; the crippled *Essex* was going nowhere. Having satisfied himself that the enemy lay in neutral waters, outside the limits of the port, he signalled *Cherub* to prepare to fight at anchor, reeving additional cables to the anchors, so the ship could be veered round to bring the broadside to bear. This was sound practice. While the crew were working on the cables George O'Brien and Mr Murphy, master of the brig *Good Friends*, boarded

Phoebe. These men were familiar with the harbour.

Hillyar held the initiative: he could sail and manoeuvre, *Phoebe* had a long-range main battery, and a more powerful second. He moved in for the kill, planning to bring his ship close under the *Essex's* stern. In the event squally weather pushed *Phoebe* further off, and when the battle began at 4.20 (3.55 on *Essex*) it was fought at half gunshot, about 250 yards. Both British ships were still underway. *Phoebe* opened with both long guns and carronades on *Essex's* stern and starboard quarter. *Cherub* fired on *Essex's* starboard bow, until heavy, accurate return fire from the long 12-pounders on *Essex's* forecastle persuaded a badly wounded Commander Tucker to shift his berth alongside the *Phoebe*. Desperate to bring his broadside guns to bear on his tormentors, Porter twice managed to get a spring on his anchor cable, but each time it was shot away. His 32-pounder carronades proved very effective during this phase of the battle. Damaging hits from heavy projectiles persuaded Hillyar to open the range, and change his tactics. During the initial exchange *Phoebe's* popular and capable First Lieutenant, William Ingram was mortally wounded, hit in the head by splinters while standing at his post alongside the Captain. He was a tall man, and this may have been his undoing.[30] At 4.40 Hillyar ceased firing, wore round and hauled off the shore, which was very close, and came to on the larboard tack. He had not observed his fire produce any effect on *Essex*. By contrast Porter could see that *Essex's* shooting, primarily from the 12-pounders in the stern, had been accurate, damaging *Phoebe's* rigging. By the time Hillyar hauled off his topsails were flying loose, the main sail was much cut up, the jib-boom damaged and fore, main and mizzen stays shot away. Once out of range *Phoebe*'s crew quickly mended the rigging and furled the mainsail. Porter's men took the opportunity to reeve a third spring on their cable.

Before renewing the battle Hillyar hailed Tucker, advising him that *Phoebe* would fight at anchor, but *Cherub* should keep underway and fire as occasion allowed. At 5.35 *Phoebe* closed in again, engaging with her bow chasers, and receiving a steady return from *Essex*. By now the wind had fallen, occasionally to a dead calm. Once again Hillyar carefully chose his position, off *Essex's* starboard quarter, where neither broadside nor stern guns would bear. This time he remained at longer range, a little under half a mile, close enough to hit the *Essex* with almost every round from his long 18-pounders, but too far off for the American carronades to be effective. Before Hillyar could reach the position where he planned to anchor the wind shifted to the landward. Porter seized one last, desperate chance to level the playing field, setting every remaining sail, cutting his cable, hoping to run alongside the *Phoebe* and board. At 5.50 Hillyar observed *Essex* cut her cable, set the jib, foresail and fore topsail. Porter's last gambit failed; once again the wind played him false, falling away even as he cut the cable. It had always been a forlorn hope, *Essex*'s shredded rigging left him with little control over the ship. Finally Hillyar had the right conditions to fight. Calm accurate fire from the British 18-pounders quickly turned the action into a one-sided demolition. *Essex* could only reply with three 12-pounders, their crews repeatedly scythed down by shot and splinters.[31] Having disabled the enemy Hillyar edged away, keeping his distance and pounding the shattered *Essex* with double-shotted guns. As *Essex*'s Sailing Master admitted, 'we were now in a most dreadful situation as the enemy hull'd us every shot and our brave fellows falling in every direction.' The American carpenter's crew, desperately trying to plug shot holes and keep the ship afloat, were wiped out. Hillyar could see his guns 'gradually becoming more destructive', his crew 'if possible more animated'. The British guns were well laid, while most of Porter's guns were disabled, and the gun crews killed. Finally the explosion of a few powder charges near *Essex*'s main hatchway broke the morale of a crew shattered by heavy loss of life and limb. Porter had to surrender, but before he did he wanted to destroy the ship, ordering *Essex* run ashore and blown up. Once again the wind let him down, and with so many badly wounded men onboard he had no option but to haul down his colours. He encouraged the able bodied to abandon ship; sixty or seventy took the opportunity. As Thornton observed: 'All the Englishmen on board of the *Essex* now jumped overboard, except for a few who attempted to save themselves by getting in a boat, & she was swamped under the stern, & they were all drowned.'[32] Some men were rescued by British boats, perhaps forty men escaping to the shore. Such was the chaos and confusion in the American rigging, and the profusion of flags and banners that Porter had hoisted that it took ten minutes for the British to realise the American colours had been lowered.[33] Hillyar sent a boat to take possession of his prize, and secure her papers.

Drained by the nervous energy required to stand on *Essex*'s shattered upper deck throughout the battle to show his men that he was not afraid, traumatised by the casualties and humiliated by defeat, Porter openly wept as he boarded *Phoebe* to offer the victor his sword. Magnanimous in victory Hillyar refused the customary gesture. The account Porter wrote of his decision to surrender, composed some three months later, implies that only a seemingly endless succession of misfortunes prevented him from capturing a nervous, beaten enemy. This reflected a remarkable degree of self-deception while the accompanying imputations of dishonourable conduct, illegal action and inhumanity cast at James Hillyar reveal Porter's anxiety that an American Court of Inquiry might not be satisfied by his explanation of how he came to lose the United States Ship *Essex*. He begged Navy Secretary William Jones to accept 'that our conduct may prove satisfactory to our country', and concluded by claiming the American Government had a right to have the ship restored.[34] Curiously, these deluded, self-serving ramblings have remained the standard version of the six-week stand off and bloody combat at Valparaiso.

In marked contrast James Hillyar praised the performance of the *Essex*, which 'did honour to her brave defenders'. Porter struck his colours only when heavy casualties and damage to his ship made further resistance futile. As he was entitled to head money for every American sailor, he was less than pleased by Porter's decision to urge his men overboard, claiming these men were, in honour, his prisoners. To make matters worse the ship's log and muster books were missing.[35] *Phoebe* lost 4 killed and 7 wounded, *Cherub* 1 and 3; in contrast *Essex* suffered 60 per cent casualties, amounting to 58 dead and 65 wounded, a heavy butcher's bill by contemporary standards. After the action both ships were perfectly seaworthy, although much cut up aloft. *Essex Junior* remained a motionless spectator throughout the battle, only joining in when it came time to surrender. Royal Marine Lieutenant Charles Sampson produced an altogether more matter of fact account, claiming the American ship was larger, which was not true, and more heavily armed, which was only true at short range.[36]

Having proved his mettle in battle Gardiner was sent to take charge of the prisoners, and then appointed to the prize. He also had an opportunity for a run ashore, although shabby Valparaiso and the 'indolence' of the inhabitants left him unimpressed. The forts were no better, badly built and poorly sited. The most important part of his text was a sound assessment of how to use the anchorage, compiled for other mariners, and in all probability based on conversations with George O'Brien. Chile was fertile, and productive, local hemp was 'the finest in the world' while meat, grain and vegetables were cheap and plentiful. For his own pleasure he composed a suitably lyrical description of the sublime vista of the Andes lit by the setting sun.

Hillyar exploited his victory by improving conditions for British trade. He sent *Cherub* to deal with any Americans that might remain in the Marquesas, and travelled to Santiago to help reconcile the Royalist Peruvian and Republican Chilean governments now that the European war had ended and Spanish power might be restored. The Treaty of Lircay proved useful, if only briefly, in promoting British trade.[37] On 21 May HMS *Briton* arrived at Valparaiso, and ten days later *Phoebe* sailed for home with her prize.[38] Admiral Dixon praised Hillyar's conduct,[39] confirmed the Treaty[40] and directed the frigates *Briton* and *Tagus* to remain in the South Pacific, along with *Cherub*, to protect British whalers from American or Peruvian privateers.[41] The American privateer *Joel Barlow* was taken by *Briton* on 3 July, completing the rout of American cruisers in Pacific waters.[42] This ended American operations in the Pacific, leaving the British to police local conflicts, and control the ever expanding local market. *Essex* made the passage round Cape Horn with a crew of only seventy, and despite having several men sick she made a fine passage to Rio. *Phoebe* and the newly commissioned HMS *Essex*, with Gardiner as Second Lieutenant, sailed from Rio on 15 September, reaching Spithead on 13 November 1814.

Initially, British accounts downplayed Hillyar's success, praising Porter and his men for their courage. Such opinions did not survive the first blast of Porter's self-serving apologia. In marked contrast, American accounts were dominated by hyperbole, reflecting a desperate need for good news. Republican Party hacks printed Porter's words, embellishing his every carping complaint. When President James Madison referred to the *Essex* in his 1814 Message to Congress, he claimed her 'loss is hidden in the blaze of heroism with which she was defended'.[43] America needed a hero: 1813 and 1814 had been disastrous years. The oceans across which American warships had roamed freely in 1812 were dominated by British convoys, blockades and patrols.

Porter had been mightily relieved to receive a hero's welcome in New York.[44] The adulation deepened his delusion. After a succession of public ovations, dinners and celebrations he began to rewrite his defeat as a victory, prompting Navy Secretary William Jones to declare that Porter and his crew returned 'in triumph though captives'. Despite the public celebrations Porter needed a Court of Enquiry to formally acquit him of blame for the loss of the ship, and he was far from certain that his conduct warranted such a judgement. Secretary Jones ordered a court, only to suspended proceedings eight days later, before a word had been spoken. He released the Captain and crew to travel south to defend Washington from British attack.[45] The Court was never reconvened. The lack of formal closure may explain why Porter published his account of the voyage, in effect putting his case before the public.[46] There was certainly a strong strain of *ex post facto* self-justification in his text, reinforced in the 1822 edition by further 'evidence' of British illegality and dishonour.[47] Although little more than a smokescreen of excuses these claims have held the field ever since. At heart Porter's complaint was that he lost the battle.

The book was written in the New York home of an old friend, author Washington Irving. Porter used it to declare himself a hero, and a successful commerce destroyer. In truth he did very little damage to British interests.[48] Despite the obvious flaws in his logic, Porter's version of the cruise of the *Essex* became a central pillar in the mythology of commerce raiding, an antecedent of the *Alabama*, the *Emden* and the *Atlantis*. All four ships were hunted down and destroyed by dominant navies whose sea control they could neither challenge nor contest. The cruise of the *Essex* proved the soundness of Secretary Jones' orders to avoid fighting enemy warships.[49] In the standard British account of the war historian William James took a studied and considered revenge on Porter, lambasting his honour and integrity, spicing his comments with evangelical outrage at his salacious tales of promiscuous liaisons with the girls of the Marquesas Islands. David Porter had a facility for making enemies; he would make many more after 1815.[50]

The Journal

While Gardiner's journal provides unique insights into *Phoebe*'s voyage and the battle in Valparaiso Bay, it also offers new perspectives on other locations and events in South America. As a junior officer Gardiner was able to get ashore at many of the landfalls that dotted the round trip from England to the coast of Peru and back. Indeed the text is dominated by events on land. Only rarely does he discuss the sea – a severe storm, the freezing temperatures encountered rounding Cape Horn, or the delays caused by doldrums and adverse weather. Gardiner approached each landing with a working knowledge of the history, politics, resources and wonders of the region. This enabled him to make good use of his time ashore, and the contacts he made there. His education at the Royal Naval College had focused on making systematic assessments of new locations. He noted the layout of the harbour, the holding ground for anchors, the risk of dangerous winds, local amenities, forts and food. Once ashore local flora and fauna are addressed, especially where they differ from that of England. He makes interesting comments on meteorology and wind systems which reflect the contemporary state of nautical science. He was quick to exploit opportunities to examine pre-Columbian archaeological sites in Peru, which he analysed with some skill. As might be expected of a young man on a long voyage the journal is full of references to women and girls, pretty, saintly or otherwise, usually compared with those back home. In Peru he was disgusted by the relish they displayed at the bullfight, and the endless smoking that ruined their teeth. His preference for the 'industrious and hardy' Chileans over the enervated inhabitants of Peru was typical. He did not expect much service from the rag-tag Lima-based Royalist army, which prove to be a sound assessment.

Gardiner's journal fits squarely into a history of naval travel writings. He was well aware of the tradition of journal writing: there would have been several on board the ship, especially those of Anson and Cook. Access to books, both a personal library and access to those of other officers, especially Captain Hillyar, would have helped to while away the long hours, and develop an understanding of the region. James Hillyar would have made it his business to assemble a useful library before sailing, and with two noted bibliophiles as Secretaries of the Admiralty in John Wilson Croker and John Barrow it is unlikely he would have been short of suggestions. Barrow was a leading figure in the world of travel writing, both as an authority on China and South Africa, and the lead reviewer in the *Quarterly Review*. A seat on the Council of the Royal Society, and close ties to Sir Joseph Banks, reinforced the link between scientific travel and naval operations.[51] Gardiner's reference to Zarate's sixteenth-century account of the conquest of Peru, which was available in a near contemporary English translation, certainly implies that some care had been taken. Returning to Rio Gardiner made the useful observation that the city seemed much improved over his previous visit from the simple fact that he had arrived from Valparaiso, rather than England. The evangelical nature of his faith was obvious from his complaints about the licentious dancing at the opera. At least the timber stands were impressive, and strategically useful. Gardiner wrote well, had a fine ear for the music of language, a solid taste in poetry and some ability. His lyrical description of the ice-encrusted *Phoebe* rounding Cape Horn repays study.

Juan Fernandez

Among the many striking passages in Gardiner's journal one of the most interesting concerns the week *Phoebe* and the ship sloops *Racoon* and *Cherub* spent at Juan Fernandez, at the island of Más a Tierra, ('closer to the shore') between 11 and 18 September 1813. The ship had passed the outer island of Más Afuera the previous day; both were excellent seamarks, their high mountain peaks often ringed by clouds. Gardiner, and it may be inferred, his fellow officers, knew the history of island, the marooning of Alexander Selkirk, the role his story played in Daniel Defoe's brilliant creation Robinson Crusoe (for whom the island was named in 1966) and the harrowing voyage of Commodore Anson's expedition, which had been saved by a prolonged residence at this magical, healthy place where scurvy would be cured and shattered ships refitted. Gardiner's poetic reading included the works of William Cowper, author of 'Monarch of all I Survey', a psychological study of Selkirk's solitary existence. A thorough reading of Anson's voyage led *Phoebe*'s offices to expect a difficult passage round the Horn. These texts were onboard the ship, as Gardiner demonstrated in his discussion of Anson's planting of peach trees, his assessment of the goat population and fish stocks. At the same time Gardiner provides an early example of the curious melding of the stories of Selkirk and Crusoe. He was told about several Selkirk caves, in different parts of the island. Selkirk lived in a grass hut close to Cumberland Bay, so any caves were Robinsonian inventions.

Typically, Gardiner recorded local defences, the difficulty of getting into Cumberland Bay, the holding ground, watering facilities and food stuffs before heading into the familiar territory of cultural relativism. Like many Englishmen of his day Gardiner felt the title to the island had long been 'the subject of speculation', dismissing the legal value of the 'wretched' Spanish occupation on Cumberland Bay, where the houses were inferior to those he had seen on Madagascar, an island ripe for colonisation. Juan Fernandez had been used as a penal colony for many years, using as guards the garrison installed to prevent a repeat of Anson's occupation. Unimpressed by this rag-tag garrison and the badly sited gun positions, he concluded 'nature is their greatest defence'. He implied that if the British were to take control 'the whole island is capable of being very strongly fortified', and could 'be made a most delightful spot'. While the Governor and his saintly daughter made a positive impression on Gardiner, the convicts and soldiers alike were noted only for indolence and dishonesty.

During the visit Captain Hillyar had the bay surveyed, improving on Anson's chart, for the benefit of succeeding expeditions. The British ships left on the 18th; *Racoon* sailed north, while *Phoebe* and *Cherub* headed off to hunt for the *Essex*.[52] A supply of live oxen, local vegetables and fish improved the health of the crew while the boats were ashore for several days obtaining firewood and water.[53] Hillyar's officers also compiled a fresh set of coastal perspectives.[54]

This was not the only contact Gardiner would have with the island. A few weeks after the capture of the *Essex* Gardiner recorded that the Governor of Juan Fernandez and most of the inhabitants arrived at Valparaiso. The Royalists had captured the mainland supply base at Concepcion, rendering the island untenable. Finally, when Hillyar led the four British frigates out from Valparaiso they passed the island, just in case a rumoured American squadron had rounded the Horn, before *Phoebe* and *Essex* parted company for 'old England' on 5 June. The *Phoebe*'s visit provided Captain Hillyar with an opportunity to conduct a little hydrographic research, taking soundings in Cumberland Bay, and acquiring Spanish charts during the voyage.

Gardiner was not alone in journalising contemporary Pacific voyages. In 1817 Royal Marine Lieutenant William Shilibeer published an illustrated account of the cruise of HMS *Briton*. After the capture of the *Essex*, *Briton* remained in the Pacific and became the first British warship to visit Pitcairn Island, last refuge of the *Bounty* mutineers. This exotic location gave Shilibeer ample opportunity to indulge his literary and artist talents, and his book became a minor commercial success. Shilibeer's romantic affinities were obvious: he wrote in the wake of Coleridge and Byron, Wordsworth and Southey. The *Briton* stopped at Juan Fernandez on the return leg of the cruise, arriving on 22 January 1815. Like Gardiner before him Shilibeer was looking for the island of Anson and 'the ingenious pen of Daniel De Foe', but he was looking with a more modern eye. His descriptions are qualified, slightly lukewarm: 'notwithstanding we did not find it that earthly paradise described by Lord Anson, it is exceedingly beautiful and capable of every improvement.' Like any sound romantic his sympathies were with the Chilean Patriots, painting a pathetic picture of the suffering of the political prisoners, men of quality and standing 'reduced to the lowest ebb of misery, and the very point of starvation.'[55] Shilibeer agreed with Gardiner that Cumberland Bay was 'neither commodious, nor safe', but the island was 'excessively mountainous and romantically picturesque, possessing several crystalline streams of water, and a soil of great fertility.' Clearly he had misjudged the purpose of Anson's text, preferring to sit on a rock to contemplate 'the most romantic, strange, and incomprehensible scenery which can be found in the formation of the universe', and execute a suitably workmanlike sketch of the bay and the headland.[56]

After

Gardiner's conduct during the voyage and the battle were commended by Captain Hillyar, and Admiral Dixon promoted him Second Lieutenant when he commissioned the prize at Rio in August 1814. The commission was confirmed by the Admiralty in December. At the end of the War Gardiner returned to the East Indies for two tours, and then served briefly in North America before promotion to Commander in 1826 ended his active naval service.[57] This was not for want of trying. Twice married, Gardiner took up missionary work, initially in Zululand, then among the Indians of Southern Chile and finally in Tierra del Fuego. He published a book on his work. While on a second expedition to convert the Patagonians Gardiner died of scurvy and malnutrition on 6 September 1851, close to the track the *Phoebe* took when she entered the South Pacific back in 1813. His work was commemorated by naming a missionary ship *Allen Gardiner*.[58] His old shipmate Samuel Thornton spent the rest of his active career on the East Indies Station, receiving his commission on returning home in 1819, before serving with distinction in the First Anglo-Burmese War, and earning promotion to Captain in 1827. Like Gardiner he was a published author, although in his case on the history of the East India Company.[59]

The War of 1812 soon slipped out of the British consciousness; having defeated Napoleon, the greatest warrior of the modern age, few Britons bothered to crow about defeating President James Madison. By contrast the Americans quickly wrote up a positive version of their defeat, largely to sustain the political ambitions of the incumbent Republican Party, creating a mythic victory.[60] David Porter's self-serving account of the *Essex*'s cruise formed a core element in that story. Allen Francis Gardiner's journal provides a useful British perspective on the Pacific campaign of 1813-1814 and the battle at Valparaiso.

Andrew Lambert
King's College, London

List of Illustrations

Between pages 88 and 89

Plate 1.
Portrait of Allen Francis Gardiner, from *A Memoir of Allen F. Gardiner* by John W Marsh (London 1857).

Plate 2.
An earlier victory for Hillyar and the *Phoebe*: the battle of Tamatave, 20 May 1811. *Phoebe* is second in the British line, and among the French frigates taken was the *Renommée*, which was renamed *Java* in British service before being captured in Dec 1812 by USS *Constitution*. (NMM neg 2583)

The main target of *Essex*'s depredations: two South Sea whalers (note the whaleboats in davits along the broadside of the nearer ship). These are post-war vessels (from about 1830) but are broadly similar to those taken by the *Essex*. They were not heavily armed and the lower tier of 'gunports' are painted, not real. (NMM BHC3390)

Plate 3.
A miniature portrait of Captain James Hillyar by an unknown artist. (NMM F9552-001)

Captain David Porter of the United States Navy, engraved for the *Analectic Magazine*. (NMM PU3523)

Plate 4.
Plate from George Anson's *Voyage Around the World* (published 1748) with his survey of the main Juan Fernandez island. Anson's account of his epic expedition was still a prime source of information on the area for both Hillyar and Porter. (NMM F0409)

Pictorial chart of Callao, from a 1778 survey of the ports of Spanish South America by Luis de Surville. Note that the map is oriented with South at the top. (NMM F2001)

Plate 5.
A chart of the Galapagos Islands by Captain James Colnett, originally surveyed in 1793 and published in 1798; this version is corrected to 1832. Both Hillyar and Porter had copies of Colnett's work on board. (NMM F0036)

Plate 6.
Gardiner was not the only British sailor to be struck by the effects of light on the Andes. This watercolour by Captain Edward Fanshawe records the spectacular sunrise over the mountains as his corvette HMS *Daphne* approached Valparaiso in June 1849. (NMM PZ4612)

As *Phoebe* discovered, rounding Cape Horn was not always traumatic. Here recorded in another Fanshawe watercolour, *Daphne* made the passage under all plain sail (admittedly, from west to east) in May 1852. Nine months earlier, not far from here on the island of Tierra del Fuego, Gardiner had died from malnutrition and disease while carrying out missionary work among the Indians. (NMM PZ4670)

Plate 7.
Essex and her prizes at Nuka Hiva in November 1813. Supposedly copied from an original in Porter's papers, this drawing is very similar to the engraved version published in Porter's *Journal of a Cruise*. The short-lived settlement was named Madisonville. (Naval Historical Center NH66426)

A view of Valparaiso Bay in the middle of the nineteenth century, looking west; coloured sketch by Harry Edgell. (NMM PX3558)

Plate 8.
A chart of Valparaiso Bay, as surveyed by the officers of HMS *Beagle* in 1835. The final battle took place in the cove, top right, between Piedra and Gorda Points, well outside the confines of the anchorage. (NMM L5760)

The final stage of the battle: the crippled *Essex* is at centre with *Phoebe* to the left and *Cherub* right. An undated watercolour by the English artist William Burley. (Beverley R Robinson collection BRR74.38)

A JOURNAL

of the

PROCEEDINGS

of

H. M. S. PHOEBE

during

A VOYAGE

to the

SOUTH SEAS

Commencing

MARCH 25 1813

By

ALLEN FRANCIS GARDINER

Prosperous zephyrs constant blow
Heaven protects where e're we go
O! guide our little bark, & bless
Each undertaking, with success,
Be ours to lead the way to fame
Emulate each glorious name

The principal object of this voyage of which I intend to give a short account, is to take possession of an American Settlement on the North West Coast of America, and to intercept the trade which is carried on between that place and China.

It had long been considered as worthy of the attention of government, and upon the breaking out of the present war with the United States, was much urged by the directors of the North West Company, however on account of various delays, no necessary measures were taken till February 1813 when it was determined that the *Phoebe* should be dispatched on this service, together with the *Isaac Todd* ship of eighteen guns, which was fitted out as a letter of marque.[1] Besides her own, she was ordered to take several months provisions for us, which with the quantity of water, and articles for traffic [*ie* trade] she had on board, not only lumbered her very much, but entirely spoilt her sailing. Two of the directors of the N.W. Company, with several artificers, and mechanics, were sent on board her; and everything being ready we sailed from Spithead on the 25th of March.

As our orders were secret, the general object of the expedition was all we knew, the intermediate places of rendezvous, and our subsequent operations were all matters of conjecture. This is one of the greatest inconveniences of a sailor's life, but secrecy is a policy in war without which, even the best concerted plans must fail of success. The winds being light we moved but slowly down channel which, as may well be supposed, gave time for many of those painful reflections which though pride often conceals, nature cannot suppress.

Fortune seemed to smile upon us even at this early period of our voyage, for scarcely had we lost sight of old England's shores, than we discovered two ships to leeward in chase of third, and making all sail after them, soon came up with, and even in time to share for the capture of *La Meglionesse*, French Corvette of 20 guns, and 140 men.[2] She had only been two days from Brest, and had made no captures. The other two ships were the *Unicorn* and *Stag*, which had been in chace of her nearly the whole morning.

Our first orders were now opened by which we were directed to steer for the Island of Teneriffe, there to complete our water, and from thence to proceed to Rio Janeiro, where we should open our final orders. Soon after we got out of the channel we encountered a strong gale from the NE which did not however last long, but decreased into a steady breeze from that quarter, and notwithstanding the bad sailing of the *Isaac Todd* we made Teneriffe on the morning of the 11th. The height and ruggedness of this island whose cloud capt mountains are perpetually covered with snow had a very remarkable appearance on our nearer approach and many of the latter from their abruptness and wild irregularity bore evident marks of having been of volcanic production. Had this island been as well known to the Ancients as the neighbouring coast, Atlas no doubt would have long since been eased of his ponderous burden.[3]

We anchored in Santa Cruz bay in the Evening, where we found the *Doris*, *Salcette*, and *Porcupine* with all the East India fleet.[4] This harbour or rather roadstead is very insecure, being completely open and unsheltered to the Southward and is seldom free from a heavy swell which occasions a great surf on the beach.

As all the best births which are nearly opposite the town about ¾ of a mile from the shore, were occupied, we were obliged to anchor farther out, where we had 50 fathoms, and moored with the kedge to the Southward.

The town is situated nearly at the head of the bay, on a gentle ascent at the foot of a high mountain. The country around and many of the hills are well cultivated and produce corn, grapes, and figs, but a great deal is necessarily left barren on account of the ruggedness of the rocks and the difficulty of access.

The town from its romantic situation has a pretty appearance from the bay, but the houses are low, ill built, and irregular, few of them exceeding two stories. In this small town there are three churches, which are very conspicuous, two of them in particular being considerably higher than any of the other buildings, and when entering the bay, had the appearance of ships at anchor. In one of these are still preserved, as trophy's of war, two English Jacks, which were taken when the fort was attacked by Lord Nelson, and a cross is erected on the place where he attempted to land.[5]

Our meeting with the India fleet made our stay here very pleasant. The number of passengers they had on board, and particularly those of the female sex, did not a little enliven the scene; and add to our amusement.

But yet amidst all this happiness and similarity of feeling which seemed to reign in every breast, there was one among us, who looked upon these things in a far different light and whose story I think cannot fail to draw a tear of sympathy. This was a native of Santa Cruz, who had been nineteen years in our service, but had never since his first entry, had an opportunity of visiting his native place, or even of hearing of any of his friends. Immediately on our arrival here, he asked permission to go on shore, stating the circumstances, which was readily granted. But only conceive the agitation of a mind employed in such a distressing research, uncertain what misery another hour might disclose. He returned on board the same evening, but what was the result? His parents who were both living when he left the Island had long since paid the debt of nature, all his friends had left the place, nor could he hear any account of the remainder of his unfortunate family. This though a sad, is not a solitary instance of the complicated misfortunes which often attend the sailor on his return to his native country, but from their long absences and the few opportunities which they have even when on shore of visiting their friends, they are often led to anticipate these trying events.

> * "Then happy those—since each must drain
> "His share of pleasure share of pain—
> "Then happy those beloved of heav'n
> "To whom the mingled cup is given
> "Whose lenient sorrows find relief
> "Whose joys are chastened by their grief."

We were much disappointed at not being able to see the Peak before we sailed from Santa Cruz bay which is on the N.E. end of this island; it cannot be seen on account of the surrounding high land, and when we sailed, which was on the evening of the

---

*Scott's Marmion

15th, the darkness of the night concealed it from our view. The East India Convoy sailed the same morning but two of them (*Ocean* and *De Vaynes*)[6] not being quite ready we took them under our convoy, expecting to join the fleet at the Cape de Verd Islands from which we intended to take a fresh departure.

We fell in with the N.E. trades two days before we arrived in Santa Cruz, but on account of the frequent calms and light winds which we now experienced, together with the bad sailing of the convoy did not make the Cape de Verds till the morning of the 26th.

At day light we saw St Antonio which is the westernmost of the group, but as the weather was very hazy the high, and apparently barren, summit of this island was all that we could at that time distinguish, rising as it were majestically above those mists which entirely concealed its base. This is frequently the case in these climates, occasioned by the great exhalations which the powerful, and almost perpendicular, rays of the sun, always produce.

Imagining that the India Fleet were astern, and supposing that they would touch here, we lay too till the morning in expectation of seeing them, that we might resign our charge, but being disappointed we again continued our course to the Southward, passed the small island of Brava, and the next night saw the volcano on Fogo. The sky was particularly clear and the moon had just then risen, so that although at a great distance it could be seen very distinctly. The next day we passed within a few miles of this Atlantic Lemnos, whose wild, and mountainous, appearance agreed in every respect with the picture which imagination had drawn the night before. We now bade adieu to the old world and were looking forward with pleasure to the time of our arrival in Rio Janeiro which was to be the next place of rendezvous.

Nothing particular occurred till the 5th of May, when being within 5° of the line, an interesting, though trivial circumstance gave rise to many pleasing reflections, which although equally transient with their pinioned excitor, I should be sorry to pass over in silence. They were occasioned by the unexpected appearance of a solitary swallow, who followed us for some time and by its slow and mournful movements seemed to solicit our protection. After flying several times round the ship as though unwilling to approach, without some assurance on our part, it at length alighted, and hopping about from one rope to the other, seemed to share in the general amusement.

But sailors who on many occasions display a generous feeling, perhaps peculiar to themselves, yet seldom evince it by those soothing methods which alone can afford relief to the distressed objects of their benevolence. Under such mistaken notions of kindness they were determined to catch this little wanderer following it from one place to another till at last weary of such inhospitable treatment though perhaps not less weary of its long journey it left us as quickly as Noah's dove when she found no rest for her foot. It is to be hoped that it found an ark in some of our convoy but I fear not.

I have only hinted as to the pleasing reflections which this little incident occasioned, but as I can only judge of those which passed in my own breast I shall be silent. Suffice it to say that such are accidental and unexpected visit from a bird of its domestic nature and so common in England could not fail to present to a <u>sea-green</u> imagination, many of those rural and social scenes, kind friends, and affectionate relations whose influence on the mind only increases as distance separates.

From this time we were almost continually becalmed for nearly a fortnight, when being in about 3° north, the long wished for breeze at length sprung up from the Southward, and brought us into the S.E. trades. We crossed the line early on the morning of the 15th, in Longitude 22°, and went through the usual ceremonies of ducking, and shaving.[7] As these seas are now so much frequented, one would suppose that this custom would be abolished, but it is still entered into with great spirit, indeed the forfeits, which are always paid in liquor by those officers who have never crossed before, are great inducements to the continuance of this tribute as it is called to Neptune, but which is generally conse-crated to Bacchus.

The *Ocean*, and *De Vaynes*, parted company on the 28th, and although we took the *Isaac Todd* in tow a few days after we crossed the line, we did not make Cape Frio till the 9th of June. On the 11th we anchored in Rio Janeiro, after a tedious passage of eleven weeks and one day.

The bold and mountainous appearance of the land about the entrance of the harbour is very remarkable, forming many high, and singular peaks, but particularly that called the Sugar loaf, which rises almost perpendicularly, and forms the Southern entrance.

This harbour which is very capacious, and able to contain the largest fleet, is interspersed with several small islands, nor have the advantageous situations of those near its mouth been overlooked by the Portuguese, as they are well fortified, and are a great addition to the strength of the place.

The city of St Sebastian which is on the Southern shore, is situated in a valley close to the sea, and from the number of churches, and public buildings which it contains, has a very pretty appearance from the bay. Although nature has drawn her outline here, with her roughest pencil, yet she has clothed it, with such exquisite colours, that its wildness only increases its beauty. The valleys are covered with verdure, and the rough summits of the highest mountains are generally softened with the most luxurious foliage.

> * "The negligence of Nature wide and wild,
> "When undisguis'd by mimic art, she spreads
> "Unbounded beauty to the roving eye."

I was however much disappointed when I went on shore, for all which from the ship had the appearance of beauty and grandeur seemed to vanish when I entered the narrow, and dirty streets of this city. Indeed I think there is no place where the very great inferiority of the works of man when compared with those of nature, is more remarkably displayed; but as Cowper justly observes,

> "God made the Country, man the Town".[9]

There are however some streets which are broad, and tolerably well built, but there is in general such an intermixture of fine houses, and miserable looking shops, that the latter destroy the effect of the former. The churches are their greatest pride, and these are indeed very neat, and richly ornamented.

Bahia, or as it is now generally called St Salvador, was formerly the capital, and is still the see of the

---

* Thompson.[8]

principal bishop of the Brazils, but the opulence and the convenient situation of this place has given it the preference, and the court has been held here for some time.

The Palace is situated on the South side of a large square facing the sea in one part of which is the Princes Chapel, and in the front a fountain dedicated to Phoebe. The water is conveyed into the town from a great distance, by means of an aqueduct, which is composed of a double row of arches one above the other; it is very conspicuous on entering the bay which no doubt must be a great disadvantage to a garrisoned town. The vain affectation of pomp and grandeur which is every-where observable among the nobility and gentry of this place, is quite ridiculous, and it is not uncommon to see them driving about in their carriages attended by two or more servants whose hats and coats are embroidered with lace, but without either shoes, or stockings. But notwith-standing all their pretensions to affluence, and state, they entirely exist on the exertions of those poor wretches whom they force from their country to supply the want of industry, and the calls of avarice. Men, women, and children, are here bought, and sold, in the market, with as much unconcern as a horse, or a sheep would be in Europe. The indolence of the inhabitants is alone sufficient to render them despicable, in the estimation of an Englishman, but

when we find them capable of such inhuman prac-
tices, they seem to sink below the very brutes.

How deplorable it is that any people who
profess christianity, or indeed have the least pretensions to civilization can so wilfully transgress
the dictates of nature, and the ties of humanity. A
few days before we sailed, the Prince paid us a
visit in his barge, accompanied by several other
boats of state, they pulled in procession round the
fleet, but only came on board the English ships
when his majesty was welcomed with three royal
salutes, and returned amidst the acclamations of
the sailors.

The tides here are very irregular, the ebb sometimes running for 36 hours and generally much
longer than the flood. This I think can only be
accounted for by the heavy rains which frequently
fall in the northern provinces, and by overflowing
the numerous rivers which discharge themselves into
the bay occasion the ebb to run much longer at
sometimes than at others. There is plenty of water,
and good holding ground in almost every port, but
the most convenient anchorage is about half a mile
from the centre of St Sebastian with the Sugar loaf
bearing S.E. where there is from 13 to 17 fathoms
but from the above mentioned circumstances
together with the usual light and variable winds,
great attention should be paid to keep a clear anchor.

The *Cherub*, and *Rackoon*,[10] having been previously ordered to accompany us and the *Isaac Todd* round Cape Horn, having now completed our water, and provisions, we weighed anchor on the 9th of July, and proceeded on the voyage with our little squadron.

For a few days we had a fine breeze from the N. E. and were all in great expectation of making a quick passage, but it soon came round to the westward, and increasing to a hard gale obliged us to lay too. The second day it moderated, but the weather became very unsettled, and we made but little progress. On the 29th though it blew strong from the northward, the atmosphere was so very thick and foggy, that in the evening notwithstanding every precaution we lost sight of the *Isaac Todd*. The next day we stood on under easy sail in expectation of seeing her, as from her usual bad sailing we supposed she must have been astern, as she did not however make her appearance, we made sail, and to tell the truth were heartily glad that we were rid of such a troublesome companion.

The Albatross and Pinladas (sic) which had been our constant companions ever since we left the Brazils, now began to desert us in great numbers, and in a few days there was not one to be seen, probably owing to the cold weather which the late westerly winds had occasioned. Such is the force of instinct which the Creator has given to these in common with all his creatures and thus not the smallest portion even of air or water is unoccupied by its proper inhabitants.

We were now advancing fast to the Southward and preparing for the bad weather which by all accounts we had every reason soon to expect, nothing however could be more favourable than it was at present, we had a moderate breeze, and a smooth sea, passing to the westward of the Falkland Islands made Staten land[11] on the 10th of August. This island which is about 40 miles in length, is one uninterrupted mass of rocks and mountains, without the least sign of vegetation, and being almost entirely covered with snow, had a most dreary, and inhospitable, appearance. Cape St Johns which is on the Eastern-most, and may readily be known by the long flat point which projects to some distance, and terminating abruptly has very much the appearance of a quay, off which is a small detached rock, which we at first mistook for a sail.

When within a few miles of this point we observed a rapid current setting to the Southward, which being in the contrary direction to the wind occasioned a great swell. We were now congratulating ourselves at having thus far escaped those storms & tempests which we had so long expected; but we had not lost sight of the land before the wind shifted to the S.W. and in a few hours increased to a strong gale. This we considered as the beginning of our troubles. All that we had heard of

Cape Horn and the violent storms so prevalent in its vicinity had in imagination already beset us, and we expected nothing less than one of those dreadful gales. In this however we were happily mistaken; a few days brought us again into moderate weather nor did it at any time blow harder than in the gale which we experienced a few days after we left Rio Janeiro. The westerly wind still continuing, we made but slow advances, and the weather became extremely cold. The frost was so severe on the 14th that in a few hours the ship was at the water mark completely encrusted with ice, but particularly about the bows when every sea added a new coat, till it became of such thickness as entirely to conceal the figure head. Madam Phoebe I am convinced was never before decked with so white a garb*. This was by far the coldest day we had and the quicksilver on deck was as low as 16°; we were then in Lat: 57° S. & Long: 62° W. On the following day being in nearly the same Longitude [presumably a mistake for Latitude] & about 65° 50 W. Longitude, it rose to 27° & although we went as far as 58° 30 S. it was seldom below 30°. The average standard was about 35° which we considered as very temperate at this time of the year. After contending with contrary winds for nearly a fortnight during which time we made but little progress, the favouring gale at length

---

*See note 1st page 158. [page 127 of this edition]

sprung up, and on the 21st we saw the islands of Diego Ramirez. These islands or rather rocks are three in number, the largest is about 2 miles in circumference but had not the least appearance of vegetation, or any other inducement for our nearer approach. They are however a good landfall as they lie to the southward of Cape Horn and all the islands on this coast. The doubling of this cape has generally been considered as a tedious, and often a dangerous undertaking, yet I cannot but think that it has been a little misrepresented. Of the former we had but little reason to complain, of the latter we saw none. That we had an excellent passage I will readily allow, but travellers and voyagers, like poets, have their licences and here I think they have exceeded their bounds, be this as it may I only hope that all who come this way for the future may have occasion to make a similar remark. We were now at length in the Pacific Ocean, but had not as yet met with those gentle breezes and unruffled seas, which former navigators have described as its characteristic and from which it obtained its name. On the 7th however after a violent gale which came on the preceding evening, the weather was materially altered. This as though the last effort of the contending elements was much more violent than any we had experienced before, but it was not of long duration and from this time we had moderate breezes & the most delightful weather.

On leaving the Brazils it was our intention after having rounded the Cape to rendezvous at Valparaiso and there take in a fresh supply of water, and provisions, but because of the westerly winds which we found so prevalent on this part of the coast, and which would probably have become light and variable as we approached the continent, we thought it most advisable to steer for the island of Juan Fernandez.

Accordingly on the 10th we passed the small island of Macafuero,[12] and at daylight the next morning were welcomed with a distant view of the spot so celebrated in the romance of Robinson Crusoe. The broken, craggy, and irregular form of this island, which is extremely high and mountainous, was very remarkable, and could not certainly be mistaken by anyone who had seen it before. We had a fine breeze from the southward and in the Evening were abreast of the Easternmost point, but hauling up towards Cumberland bay which is on the North side of the island, we were for a short time becalmed; the wind however which was obstructed by the intervening high land frequently found means to escape and rushing down the valleys in violent gusts often obliged us to reduce our sail, in this manner we beat about for several hours sometimes becalmed, and at others in heavy squalls, till at length after much trouble, and fatigue, we were obliged to come too, in 47 fathoms.

In this situation however we were much exposed, and from the sudden gusts which continually blew off the land were in great danger of drifting, we therefore took the advantage of a lull and shifted our birth within half a mile of the shore, when we had 36 fathoms and moored with an open hawse to the southward.

This island which has been so long the subject of speculation, is at length in the possession of the Spaniards, who have a small settlement in this bay. It is however in a wretched condition at present, and is only a depot for convicts who are transported from the continent. Nothing could exceed the friendly manner in which we were received by governor Don Manuel, who offered us every assistance in his power, and even warned us against the inhabitants whom we soon found to be the greatest thieves, and rogues, we had ever met with. A few days before we arrived they received some supplies by a brig from Valparaiso, which was the only vessel that had been here for nearly 18 months. They accounted for this neglect by the disturbances which had lately taken place on the continent, occasioned by the insurrection of the province of Chili, & which had involved the whole country in a state of warfare.[13]

The monopoly, and improper disposition of the wealth, and revenues of this country, were as far as we could learn the grievances alleged, and in consequence the Viceroy of Peru had collected a large army in order to force them to subjection.

Thus situated every trifling article, but particularly those of clothing, as may well be supposed, were of double value to these poor exiles, and I am willing to think that had we been here at a less critical time, we should have found more honesty among them.

On the west side of the bay is the fort, which is built on a steep ascent near the landing place, but is commanded by the adjacent hills. It is of a square form, fortified towards the sea, and contains 14 ill mounted guns, which as there is no rampart are very conspicuous, within are the houses of the soldiers and in the centre is a gallows for the accommodation of the inhabitants.

To the left of this on the continuation of the same hill are four crazy[14] pieces which perhaps they consider as a battery but as this post is not fortified even with a breast work, I shall not give it that appellation; on the right of the town, are six more nearly in the same situation, but there is a small battery of three guns on an adjoining mountain which commands the whole. The garrison consists only of 80 men, but they are so ill provided, that I question whether they could muster 80 muskets. In their present situation therefore it is evident they could not withstand the smallest attack if well directed, but nature is their greatest defence, and this bay and indeed the whole island is capable of being very strongly fortified.

The town, or rather village, for it does not contain more than 100 houses, is situated in a valley near the fort, and is the only place which is inhabited, the whole, soldiers included, do not exceed 250. This might with a little trouble be made a most delightful spot, but at present is but an asylum for indolence, and poverty. They take little pains in cultivating the land which excepting their gardens is left almost entirely in its natural state, nor do they appear to be more concerned about the construction of their houses, many of which, were falling about their ears. These, the governor's alone excepted, consist but of one room, and are built with mud a small aperture being left which answers the double purpose of window, and chimney. They are thatched over but are so rudely contrived, that I have really seen better on the coast of Madagascar.

How long this island has been inhabited we could not exactly learn, some of the people said they had been here six, and others fifteen years, the governor himself had only been five, and the chapel was built Septr. 24th 1811, so that it probably had not been many years under the protection of the Spanish government.

Although this is by far the most mountainous side of the island, yet the lands are much richer, and more productive, than in any other part. The valleys are capable of the highest cultivation, but the soil on the mountains is in general shallow and they are so difficult of access, that they must for ever remain in their natural, wild & unimproved state. Nothing could be more romantic than the scenery around us, yet we could not but regret the want of art, and industry, to assist and display with greater variety the beauties of nature.

The unfortunate man whom I had occasion before to mention having so suddenly heard of the loss of his friends when we were at Teneriffe, now became in great request, and attended us on shore on all occasions, as Spanish interpreter. Through this medium I am happy in being able to relate a little anecdote of the governor's daughter, which no doubt will give a better idea of the simplicity, and affection of this poor girl than any eulogium I might pass. A few days before we sailed the Governor expressed a wish to come on board with his family, and accordingly several officers with myself waited on him to attend them off. In course of conversation it was asked how she liked being on an island, which at her age (about 19) without amusement, or society, could not be supposed to be very agreeable. She did not however hesitate, but turning to her Father with a smile on her countenance, said, "She was happy to be any where with him." An answer so unexpected, and which at the same time portrayed so much virtue, and good sense, could not be disregarded by any of the company, and only left us to regret that so fair a jewel, which would be an ornament to any society, should be concealed in such an unfrequented abode. This good family are continually employed in acts of charity, and benevolence, and are constant attendants at a small house which is appropriated for the reception of the sick, whose necessities are in a great measure alleviated by their advice and assistance.

Many by these measures, strive to gain the applause of the world, but in this sequestered spot where there is scarcely another eye to behold, pride can have no influence; the consciousness of doing right is their only motive, and surely their highest reward.

This place is much indebted to Lord Anson for the number of Peach Trees he planted, and which now grow in great abundance in all the gardens.[15] There is very little large timber on this island, but the mountains on this side, are in general well covered with different species of myrtle, box and privet, whose lively colours form a beautiful contrast with the dark, and sombre tinges of the rocks. The only vegetables we found were turnips, radishes, and celery which grow wild in great plenty but which the inhabitants take little pains to cultivate. As for the goats, which are said to have been formerly so numerous, we did not see one, the whole race having been nearly extirpated by the number of dogs which were put on shore here, at the time of the Spanish war, for that purpose. The few that remain conceal themselves among the crags of the rocks, where it is almost impossible to catch them. Bullocks are found wild on the mountains and are caught with a noose in the same manner as on the continent, at which these people are very expert. These with a few pigs, sheep, and poultry which former, however are very rarely to be met with, are the only animals on the island. The poultry are scarce and very dear, as indeed are most other necessaries, so that upon the whole this is not a convenient place at which a ship may refresh after rounding the Cape, and had not circumstances obliged us to keep our motions as secret as possible, it would certainly have been better to have put into Valparaiso or any other port in Chili.

Cumberland bay is by far the best anchorage, but it is quite open, and unsheltered to the northward, which added to the violent gusts of winds, I have before mentioned, render it not altogether an eligible place for shipping. We found here a great abundance of fish of different kinds, but the Cod and Bream were in the greatest repute, & are by far the most numerous.

Before I leave this place I must not forget poor Alexander Selkirk,[16] although I had not an opportunity of visiting his habitation. There are however three caves on the opposite side of the island which are said to have been inhabited by him at different times, and in which his name is still to be seen cut in the rock. Those who had been there, said that they were very difficult of access, but when approached would well repay the fatigue of the journey. This account only increased our curiosity, which however, as our stay was but short, and the necessary duties of the ship urgent we were not able to satisfy.

When we were at Rio Janiero, we had intelligence that the *Essex* American Frigate was in these seas, that she had made a great number of captures, and was at that time refitting in Valparaiso. We now heard from the account brought by the brig before mentioned, that she had armed several vessels some of which had been seen cruizing off that port, so late as the 23rd of August. Nothing now remained but to go in quest of her, which we had long wished, and we gave up all idea of the Columbia. The *Raccoon* however was ordered to proceed on that service, and we determined to accompany her to the Equator, where she would most probably be out of danger of falling in with the enemy, and thus far we should ensure the success of the expedition. Our water which is filled at a spring near the landing place being now nearly completed together with the wood, and other necessaries, we began to think of sailing and on the 18th bad adieu to this place, which our people, not without reason, called the bay of thieves.

The wind was from the Southward and on the second day brought us into the SE. trades, which we found much stronger, and more steady, than we had ever known in the Atlantic, or even the Indian Ocean. Nothing particular occurred till the 29th when being on the north coast of Peru, we fell in with a Spanish brig, bound to Lima, which informed us that the *Essex* had been in the bay of Guayaquil about two months since, and had there landed a number of English prisoners whom she had taken out of our South Sea-men.[17] Upon this information we determined to steer directly for that place, where we hoped to obtain a more particular account of her proceedings, and also to relieve those poor fellows whom they told us were in great distress.

On the 2nd of October we parted company with the *Raccoon*, and hauling in for the land, made Cape Blanco the next morning. During the whole of this run from Juan Fernandez we had fine breezes, and pleasant weather, nor were we once becalmed, but what is still more remarkable we had no rain, although the sky was almost continually clouded. This deficiency is however in a great measure supplied by the heavy dews that fall in the night, and make them in general very cold. Instead of the hot, and sultry weather, so frequent in these latitudes on the other side of the continent, we were now continually refreshed by a steady & most delightful breeze, and the powerful rays of an almost per-pendicular sun, were in a great measure absorbed by the intervening clouds.

The immense expanse of almost uninterrupted ocean on the one hand, bounded by an extensive range of those prodigious mountains, the Andes, on the other, whose summits are perpetually covered with snow, are doubtless the principal causes of these salutary effects, for the wind which was before confined, and at the same time highly condensed, now meeting with no opposition, naturally rushes to those parts which are more rarefied and occasions here a more constant and refreshing current of air than is perhaps to be met with in any other part of the torrid zone. This likewise may in a great measure occasion the scarcity of rain before mentioned, for by giving the clouds a continual motion in the same direction, they cannot accumulate till they arrive to the northward of the line, when the NE. and SE. trades generally meet. Their junction is always attended with calms, and light winds and the Atmosphere not being able to support the weight of so great a body of vapours, they fall and discharge themselves in heavy torrents of rain which are said to be more frequent, and violent than in any other part of the world.

The land about Cape Blanco is high, and level with a bold shore and had very much the appearance of the Lizard point on the coast of Cornwall but as we proceeded farther to the northward, it became very low, and everywhere presented a fine sandy beach. We continued running along shore till the evening, when finding that we suddenly shoaled our water, we hauled out and brought to in 9¾ fathoms. Early the next morning we weighed with an intention of running down to St Clara, or as the Spaniards call it Muerta, but meeting with a pilot boat a few leagues from the island we were informed that it was not inhabited, and that from that station it would be difficult to beat out of the bay with the sea breeze; they also told us that on the preceding evening we had run upon a shoal, but that we were in no danger for there was everywhere from four to six fathoms, and had we gone on the other side should have found plenty of water. The best anchorage they said was off the river Tumbes, but the water would not permit us to approach within a league of the shore, accordingly we hove about, and in a few hours came to off the entrance of the river in 7 fathoms, and moored with an open hawse to the westward.

This was the first place at which Pizarro landed on the coast of Peru in 1526, and St Michaels, which is but a few leagues to the Southward, was the first Spanish Settlement of which he was the founder.

The accounts given us by the Spanish brig respecting the enemy were now authenticated. The *Essex* had been here in the latter end of July, but they could not give us any certain information concerning their subsequent proceedings. It was however generally supposed that she was either at the Gallipagoes, or cruizing to windward, off the coast of Chili. They had expected us here for some time, and orders had been issued all along the coast to supply us with every provision. The greater part of the prisoners, we found, had been sent to Lima, a number had volunteered on board a Spanish Privateer, and a few yet remained at Guayaquil. A dispatch was immediately sent to the governor of that town, acquainting him with our arrival, and requesting him that he would send them to us as soon as possible. In a few days an answer returned with four Englishmen; who informed us that the Governor was using all his endeavours to collect our people. We did not find this, by any means, a convenient anchoring place, we lay at a great distance from the shore, and at a far greater distance from any habitation. The entrance to the river is intricate, and often dangerous, and can only be approached by a small passage between two extensive shoals, on which the sea breaks with great violence.

These at low water are nearly dry, which very fortunately happened to be the case the first time our boats went on shore, and enabled us to sound in the passage. We filled our water about two miles from the entrance, which we found to be clear and excellent and completed without meeting with any accident, excepting that the last boat upset on the bar. The people however were all providentially saved. The shore here, is in general low, and sandy, and the trees grow close to the water's edge, which make a famous retreat for the Alligators, and Guanas[18] which infest this part of the coast, but particularly the rivers in great numbers. The latter are a species of Alligator though much smaller, and its flesh is held in great estimation by the inhabitants, who prefer it to almost any other kind of food. We often amused ourselves with firing at them, but the skin of the Alligator is so extremely tough, that it cannot be penetrated even by a musket ball. The belly is soft, and vulnerable, but the only sure mode of killing them is to watch an opportunity when they are asleep, which is generally with their mouths open, and fire directly down their throats, which will at once dispatch them.

Of birds we saw a great variety, the most remarkable were Pelicans, Bustards, Flamingoes, Storks, and a large kind of wild duck, besides which there were a great number of doves, paraquettes, and humming birds, with many more whose names we did not know nor am I naturalist enough to describe.

The town of Tumbes is situated on the western bank of the river, which bears its name, about fifteen miles from the entrance. A few days before we sailed I had an opportunity of visiting this place, which although it gratified my curiosity, fell far short of what I had been led to expect.

Custom, and comparison, are the great arbiters of all human ideas, and too often of their actions; but what has led me now to make this remark will presently appear in the description of this assemblage of huts, which the Indians told us was a large town. The river is narrow and the adjacent country low, and level but the banks are covered with trees of the most luxuriant foliage, which together with the numerous plantations of plantains, and bannanas, among which it meanders, have a very lively and picturesque appearance.

As this part of Peru is subject to periodical rains, these houses which are situated near the low lands, & on the banks of the river, are built of reeds, and bamboos, and raised several feet above the ground by means of stout poles on which the whole is supported. They are ascended by notches cut in the sides of one of these props, which answer the purpose of a stair case, but in the rainy season they have frequently no other method of communication one to the other than by their canoes. At a little distance from the river, is the town, which is situated on a sandy plain at the skirts of one of these plantations. The houses are miserable huts, built of mud and consist only of one or two rooms, but are in general better constructed, and more commodious than those at Juan Fernandez. The whole may amount to about 70, so that allowing five persons to inhabit each, it will give the population about 350, which cannot be far wide of the truth. The house which now answers the purpose of a church is erected near the site of the former, which was burnt down, & from its vestages appears to have been built of brick. The governor's house is constructed of the same materials as the rest, and is only distinguishable by the interior being of a dirty white, which evidently proves that it was once white washed. The interior is not more magnificent, his carpet consists of terra firma, on which is disposed a table, chest of drawers, & three or four chairs, these with a few pictures, pasted against the wall, & a mat hammock, suspended from the two sides, in which his wife occasionally swings herself to sleep, make up the whole furniture. Having given you a description of what I shall call the <u>state room</u>, you will perhaps be curious to have a peep into his excellencies chamber. In one corner is an old crazy bed, supported by two rough poles; and in another, about 30 rusty cutlasses, which, I believe, are the only weapons of defence in the whole town, the remaining space is occupied by two or three antiquated coffers, which look as if they had been part of Noah's equipage when he went into the ark. Notwithstanding these intervals, we met with a very cordial reception from the Governor and his wife, and a repast was prepared for us, consisting of fish, and eggs, which was no doubt the best they could procure. This Lady, who was by far the prettiest woman in the town, yet by no means a beauty, did not forget the licence of her sex; and was not a little loquacious. Our slight knowledge of the Spanish Language would not permit us to make ourselves very agreeable, however with the assistance of my lady, we made it out tolerably well. Thus much will suffice to give a short sketch of <u>Peruvian Poverty</u>; which at first sight would be thought almost a paradox, and would scarcely be credited were it not supported by facts. But in this country as in old Spain, there is no medium between rich, and poor: the one live upon & are in entire possession of the persons & properties of the other.

The day before we arrived here, was a holiday, and festival among the Indians, of whom this town, and the neighbouring country chiefly consist, and which they kept up with great rejoicings the whole of the evening. They were all dressed in a most singular and ridiculous manner, with silk mantles, feathers in their heads, silver caps on their knees, & looking glasses on their breasts. Some wore masks and others had their faces painted. The long knives they use in the plantations served them for swords, the blade being covered with paper, and painted red. Some used cross bows, and others tomahawks, but all held in the left hand a little effigy of a woman, probably the Virgin Mary. Thus equipped, they formed several companies, and went about the town performing, rather their dancing to the sound of a drum, and fife, which were both played by one man. The fife was held in the left hand, and the drum was suspended from the same arm and beaten with a stick in the right. To this simple music they moved round in a circle, keeping tune with their feet, and exerting every limb with an expression, and grace, which we little expected to find among these rude people. The whole seemed to be engaged in a serious conflict, and often placed their swords on the neck of the little figure they held in their hands, the meaning of which, we could not learn but concluded that it was some religious superstition. There is a cross erected between the church and the Governor's house, and this seemed to be the favorite spot for their sacred comedians, who danced around it for some time, they did not however seem to be under any restraint, but in the interludes drank freely of aquadiente, and other spirituous liquors, which were presented them from all parts.

Before I leave this place, I must not forget, the old priest's mother, whom I had an opportunity of visiting in one of my rambles. She was a fine, interesting, old woman, and appeared extremely grateful for a few Spanish Testaments and other religious books which the Captain had sent her. She seemed quite delighted to see me, desired me to sit by her side, & would scarcely quit my hand from the time I went in, till I bid her adieu. Her younger son who was unwell laid on a couch on one side of the room, and her daughter, a lively and pleasing looking girl, seemed only to wait an opportunity of rendering assistance to both. A scene so interesting, and so gratifying, had in idea transported me to my native country, and when I quitted it, could not but reflect that many of <u>our</u> priests might take a lesson from these poor catholics. I am sorry I had not an opportunity of seeing the old man, who was not at home; but as it was getting late we were obliged to retire to our boats; where we slept for a few hours, and returned to the ship the next morning.

A sudden, and melancholy accident now took place on the morning of the 9th which at once snatched three of our shipmates from time, into eternity. Mr Jago the 3rd Lieut., and Mr Surflen the Purser, had proposed going on the same expedition from which we had just returned, but a wise and all powerful Providence had determined differently. They had not long left the ship when we observed the boat swamp on the bar, and before we could get to her assistance, these two poor fellows, together with Joseph Finley, one of the boat's crew, were all unhappily drowned. Such is the uncertainty of this life, which we cannot be too well prepared to quit: but a few days before, I had been myself in the same situation, and they were the first to congratulate me on my return. But

> "God moves in a mysterious way
> "His wonders to perform"[19]

and when we think ourselves most secure, we are often in the most imminent danger.

* "No warning given! unceremonious fate!
   A sudden rush from life's meridian joys
   A hapless wat'ry bed! a plunge opaque
   Beyond conjecture! Feeble natures dread!
   Strong reason shudders at the dark unknown!
   A sun extinguished! a just opening grave!
   And oh! The last, last —-what? (can words express
   Thought reach?) the last, last—silence of a friend."

About this time a dispatch arrived overland, by which we were informed that the *Essex* had been seen off the coast near Lima, about 10 days since. No time was therefore to be lost, and we did not think it advisable to wait any longer for the remainder of the prisoners, who might not probably come down for some days, we therefore unmoored, and on the next evening (the 14th) took our leave of these melancholy scenes, with emotions scarcely to be described.

We shipped our course directly for the Gallipagoes, where we thought we should most probably meet with her, being the only place at which she could get provisions on this part of the coast, all the ports of Peru having been shut against her. During the run, we found the trades became

---

*Young's *Night Thoughts*.[20]

more Southerly, generally blowing from the S.b.W. but we had constantly a fine steady breeze, and the most delightful weather. On the 21st we made the Southernmost part of Albemarle island,[21] which we passed to windward and the next day bore up to reconnoitre Elizabeth Bay. This is the general rendezvous for all the Whalers in these seas, but we found it quite deserted as the greater part of them had been captured. In the middle of this extensive bay is situated the island of Narborough, by which two distinct roadsteads are formed, the one called Weather, and the other la baye, in neither of which however we were happy enough to meet with the enemy. This island and indeed all the Capes, and headlands we passed had very much the same appearance, rising inland to a great height, and shelving gradually towards the sea. Albemarle is by far the largest of this numerous cluster, but they are in general so barren, and uninviting that none of them have ever been inhabited, few of them afford any water; at James' island[22] however, there is a small stream, where the south sea men in general complete. Nature however has not been altogether deficient, for the greater part abound with turpins, turtles, penguins, & seals; the former of which often grow to a prodigious size, usually weighing from 400, to 700 pounds. These are the only refreshments which they afford, but are particularly excellent after a long voyage, and are still more valuable in a country where salt provisions cannot be procured.

Narborough, or perhaps as it might be more properly called Fuego, is an entire volcano, the whole summit of which is often at night seen in a blaze. At the time we passed it, the smoke was still rising from the Southernmost part, & from its black and uneven appearance bore evident marks of having been subject to frequent eruptions.

The men whom we took on board at Tumbes, had often been on shore there, and said that the surface was every where so broken by precipices, pits, and caverns, some of which were of considerable depth, that it was almost impossible to proceed far; and that from the immense cavities, the earth resounds at almost every step; which they compared to walking on a drum. I am sorry I am not able to give a more particular account of these islands, and their natural curiosities, but our present situation would not allow of the smallest delay and having been disappointed in not finding our American friends, we hauled to the wind, without even sending a boat on shore, and made sail with an intention of proceeding immediately to Lima. Had the same wind continued which brought us here, we might have looked forward to a less fatiguing passage than now seemed to be unavoidable; but having become more easterly, we were obliged to make a long stretch to the southward, and westward. Nothing particular occurred till the evening of the 28th, when

Joseph Eves, a marine, unhappily fell overboard; the ship was immediately hove too & boats lowered down, but, through the darkness of the night, all our efforts to save him were ineffectual. This is the fourth who has been drowned during the short space of three weeks, but when we compare our losses with whose of other ships that have come into these seas, we surely have great reason to be thankful.

The S. Easterly wind continuing, we were driven considerably to the westward, and were obliged to stand on to the 26° of Lat. before we could turn our heads again to the northward. In this part of our passage we had several calms & heavy showers of rain, which evidently prove that the Andes have little or no effect on the Atmosphere at this distance from the coast. After beating about for nearly six weeks, during which time we were reduced to 2/3 allowance, the wind at length shifted to the S. E. & on the 3rd of December we anchored in Callao roads. Nothing perhaps could have given us greater joy: from want, we were now surrounded with plenty, and the few sick which yet remained rapidly recovered. The report which was in circulation respecting the *Essex* when we were at Tumbes, we now found to be entirely false. She had been seen off this port about five months ago, but had sailed from Valparaiso with all her prizes (19 in number) some time since. No expedition could have been better planned, or have been crowned with greater success.

She came into these seas before the intelligence of the war arrived, captured the greater part of our southseamen, and warned all her own, off the coast. Had we been here but two months sooner we might probably have put a stop to the whole, but we now gave up all hope of meeting her.

We found here two Spanish Sloops of war, and about thirty sail of merchant ships, most of which had been employed in importing corn, and cocoa, from Chili, but which since the insurrection of that country have been laid up.

The roadstead is completely open, & exposed, yet it is the most secure, and perhaps the most commodious of any on the coast, for it never blows hard, & the largest fleet might ride here with the greatest safety. The merchant ships generally lay about ½ a mile from the shore, where they have from three to six fathoms water, and a fine muddy bottom. The land and sea breezes are regular, setting in from the S.E. and N.N.W. and are generally attended with a southerly swell, therefore to prevent getting a foul hawse, a stern-fast should be laid out to the NW. About three miles to the southward of the anchorage are two high, barren, sandy, islands, which are in some measure a security against the above mentioned swell, and are an excellent land mark, when making this port. The largest, called Lorenzo, is about two miles in length, to leeward of which, there is a good anchorage and an enemies fleet might there securely lay out of the reach of the batteries at Callao. Between these islands, & the main shore was formerly a passage for large ships, but since the earthquake in 1747, it has become so extremely intricate, as only to be practicable for very small vessels.

Callao, the port of Lima, is a small, miserable, ill built, town, little calculated to give a stranger any idea of the opulence and supposed grandeur of that city. The houses were low, few of them exceeding the ground floor, and are in general built of mud, which they use instead of plaister. The roofs are flat, and covered with mats, bamboo or other light materials, which is universal throughout this part of the country, where it never rains; and they are in continual dread of earthquakes. This town stands nearly on the site of the former, which was entirely destroyed. Some of the ruins however may still be traced, among which several human skulls, and bones, have been found, and may yet be seen in different parts of the town. The former was much larger, and more populous, containing several churches, and other public buildings, whereas now the whole population, garrison included, does not, I suppose, exceed 700. The town and roadstead are well defended, on the right by a square fort, with four bastions, and on the left by a half moon redoubt, the former mounting about 120 guns, and the latter 12. To the right of these, there is also another small redoubt of 6 guns, fortified to the southward; the square fort, called the castle, is surrounded by a ditch and, contains two martello towers,[23] which command the whole, and the road to Lima for some distance, but as the surrounding country gradually rises and the bay is every where open, and in many places accessible, it would be no object to an enemy, who would land any number of troops out of reach of the batteries and march directly to Lima.

From this description of Callao I dare say my readers will have no objection to change the scene to one more interesting and accompany me to the metropolis of Peru, which as there was little doing on board, we had all frequent opportunities of seeing.

Lima is situated about six miles to the N.E. of the port, in a spacious plain, bounded by a ridge of mountains which gradually rise till they are lost in the Andes. The road from Callao is broad & perfectly strait, and was made by order of O'Higgins the former Viceroy.[24] The country, for the first two, or three miles, is open, and uncultivated, being in general covered with a kind of heath, but as we advanced farther, it bore a more pleasing appearance, being prettily laid out in fields, and pastures. At a little distance on each side of the road may be seen some remains of the ancient Rimac, which by the extent of the ruins, must have been a place of some consequence. On the right about a mile and a quarter from Lima, is the temple of Rimac, which is dedicated to the Sun; and from which the neighbouring river takes its name. Part of the walls which were built of mud, are still perfect, but as architecture was little studied by the ancient Peruvians, beauty must give place to antiquity. The approach to the city is handsome, the last mile of the road lying between a double avenue of trees, terminated by a Gothic archway. Such an entrance in every respect agreed with the ideas we had formed of the magnificence of this place, and although we did not expect to find the streets paved with silver, we were much disappointed on our entry at its mean, and shabby appearance. Indeed they pay little attention to the exterior decoration of their houses, which are by no means inviting. They are however very commodious, and well adapted to the climate. They are all built nearly in the same manner, in the form of a square. The sitting rooms are in the centre; on each side is an open court, round which are disposed the bedrooms and the entrance from the street is by a large archway which leads into the outer court. This mode of building, renders them extremely cool, as there is a constant draught through the whole, but would be very inconvenient in any other part of the country, where they are subject to heavy rains. As the climate will not allow them to have much furniture, its place is in some measure supplied by various paintings in imitation of tapestry, and wainscoating with which most of their rooms are decorated, and has a very pretty effect. Public accommodations are very bad, the inns are vile, & beds scarcely to be procured. The fact is every stranger who comes here, immediately provides himself with lodgings, which we at length found, to our cost, would have been by far the best plan. The former in consequence are little resorted to, and will scarcely repay the landlord. Although there is nothing in the appearance of this city, the churches excepted, either grand, or interesting, it is perhaps the most regularly built and best laid out of any in the world. The streets are of good size, perfectly strait, and cross each other at right angles, those leading from the main road, running about N.N.E. & S.S.W. The whole is surrounded by a rampart, and parapet of mud about 20 feet high, with bastions at equal distances. This is however destitute of guns, and of such weak construction, that I scarcely think it would be a sufficient defence against a party of Indians. Indeed a few heavy showers of rain would demolish the whole. It was built by subscription a few years ago, and is so far of great utility as it prevents thieves and smugglers, from escaping unobserved. Every part of the city is well watered by the Rimac, which runs through it, this river is connected with the Amazon, but its rise and fall, are in a great measure in influenced by the melting of the snow on the Andes, which was even observable during the short time we were here. The bed is very broad, and before we left the place, we had the pleasure of seeing it almost entirely filled, it is however very shallow, and so extremely rapid as not to be navigable even for the smallest boat. The walls do not extend beyond the river, but that part of the city which lies on the opposite bank is connected by a neat stone bridge thrown over with three arches. The palace is situated on the north side of a large square, nearly in the middle of the city, on the right of which is the cathedral, the other two are composed of shops, and private houses. Here the market is constantly held, & in the centre is a bronze font, much celebrated for its curious workmanship but at present is in bad repair.

The palace is a shabby building without ornament and has more the appearance of a warehouse than the residence of a Viceroy. The ground floor towards the street is occupied by different trades men, but particularly shoemakers, so that it may well be said that he presides over the <u>soles </u>of his subjects. This I suppose is by way of security and thus far is a political measure, but by no means an elegant appendage. The cathedral is a handsome building, adjoining to which is the Archbishop's palace. The inside is hung with velvet, and richly adorned with gold, and silver. There are six parish churches, besides those belonging to monasteries, and a great number of chapels of smaller note. They are not built after any regular mode of architecture, being a kind of medley of ancient & modern, which are often ridiculously blended. Within they are all arranged nearly in the same manner. The whole length is divided into a nave and two aisles at the head of which are three magnificent altars. On each side of the aisles are the shrines of the different saints all richly ornamented and loaded with gold & silver. There are no windows in the sides but light is admitted by circular apertures in the roof, which leaves more room for the altars of which there are generally five of a side. St Domingo is by far the handsomest, the altars are magnificent, and the roof which is vaulted, & elegantly painted. Indeed this church alone, when completely dressed for high mass, is supposed to contain more than a million & a half Sterling. These expenses are defrayed by legacies, and donations which are thrown in from all quarters, and such is the superstition of these people (the Creoles in particular) that they will often sacrifice half their fortunes to decorate a shrine.

The archbishopric is for life, with a salary of £15,000, which is equal to that of the Viceroy besides which he has annual presents from each diocese, which generally amount to about £3,000 more.

Public amusements here are very few besides the play, which is a wretched performance, a ball, or some times a bull fight, they have no way of directing their time, or rendering the confinement of a town agreeable. In the evening however they generally resort to the public walks, of which there are several, some in the avenues before mentioned near the entrance of the city, and others on the opposite side near the river. The Viceroy and his daughter constantly attend, and they are crowded with the carriages of the nobility, & gentry (but more especially of a Sunday Evening) who come here to see and be seen. These walks are handsome, and, with the least attention, might really be made beautiful. There is nothing with which nature has not amply supplied them, trees, brooks, mountains, & cascades, all lie neglected around them, but such is the selfishness, & indolence of these people that they would rather squander away thousands to keep up an empty show, than to contribute the smallest sum to beautify their city. At a little distance are the public baths, which are thirty in number, very large, and so contrived, that a stream of running water passes through the whole. This however is the greatest objection, and it would have been much better had it been introduced separately into each, which might easily have been done were they built in a contrary direction.

There is one part of the economy of this place, which is highly worthy of imitation, and even in more temperate climates would not be without its salutary effects. I mean the strict prohibition from burying any person within the precincts of the city.

About two miles and a half distant there is a large enclosure, occupying several acres, where they are all interred. At the entrance is a chapel, which is a small, but neat building, and well appropriated to the place. Over the door, on one side, is the figure of time with his glass at a stand, and on the other a woman is represented weeping, with this inscription. "A tribute from the living to the dead." Having thus far been decoyed from the bustle of the Town, I will take this opportunity of revisiting my favorite spot which is at the back of those avenues which lead by the side of the river. From this point of view the city has the most pleasing appearance, all the shabby looking houses are concealed by the intervening trees, among which the towers and domes, majestically rise, and the whole has very much the appearance of Oxford when viewed from the road. There I have often in imagination been transported while contemplating these delightful scenes, and have indulged myself in a train of those ideas, which absence often involuntarily produces. If such are the effects which a mere affinity of nature is capable of exciting what must be those of the mind?*

But to return on board – on the 13th the Viceroy, and his daughter with several attendants paid us a visit, which was rather an unusual thing, as it is contrary to his instructions, to go on board any ship.

---

*See Note 2nd page 159. [page 127 of this edition]

They seemed however very much entertained. After dinner the ladies danced, and in the Evening returned after being previously welcomed with four royal salutes. The Viceroy is a fine venerable looking old man and about 63. He has been here rather more than seven years, although five is the stipulated time, at the expiration of which they are generally superceded from old Spain. His daughter, who is his only child, is a pretty young girl, about sixteen, and as she was the first lady we had seen on board since our arrival in this part of the world, did not fail to leave some impressions in most of our hearts. Several invitations were given as to the Palace, and on the 20th a public dance on our account which I had the honor of attending. The appartments of the Viceroy were ill furnished, and by no means answered our expectations, but what we conceived wanting of pomp, and magnificence, was more than compensated by the friendly and cordial reception we met with. I cannot but here mention a curious circumstance which happened at dinner, of which we had heard, but never before had an opportunity of witnessing. Some of the gentlemen took the liberty of sending away several dishes from the table to their friends, this we considered as a great piece of indecorum, but when we mentioned our surprise, were informed that it was a common practice though I should think a very inconvenient one. They have however a little more decency than the Italians, who I am informed frequently pocket the plate, & silver spoons, after an entertainment. After dinner we went to the circus where we saw a bull fight, which I shall describe at large as it is a favorite Spanish amusement, and will give some idea of the state of civilization in this country. The building is perfectly round, with a diameter of about 400 feet, & although not very elegant, is well contrived, having five rows of boxes one above another which well contain between eight and ten thousand people. On these occasions Lima is all in a bustle, the avenues are crowded, and every one is anxious to gain admission, which generally occasions a great press at every door. The seat appropriated for the Viceroy is much larger than any of the others, and when he makes his appearance is always attended by a strong guard; which at these times is a necessary precaution in case of any disturbance.

Each bull is ushered in separately, having been previously bred for the fight, and decorated with trappings of gold & silver, often to a considerable amount. They do not dispatch them immediately, but to heighten the sport irritate them almost to madness. The modes of attack are different, some-times on horseback, and sometimes on foot, with spears, javelins, swords, or even stilettos, which they use indiscriminately. They are very expert horsemen, and show a great deal of dexterity in the use of their mantles in which their safety almost entirely depends. With these they set him at defiance, till he makes a run at them, when by presenting the cloak & immediately jumping aside, they not only avoid the danger, but confuse the animal. The horrid scene of cruelty, & barbarism which now follows, is almost too shocking to relate, and reflects but little to the humanity of the spectators; but what concerned me the most, was to observe the same degree of pleasure & satisfaction portrayed even in the countenances of the ladies, of whom I had a much better opinion. Not contented with seeing him run through and through with spears, and swords, panting for breath, and covered with blood, as though desirous to add to his tortures, they ham string him by cutting the tendons of his hind legs. They then exultingly get upon his back, and in this situation oblige him to carry them about for several minutes, till by loss of blood he is rendered so weak, as to no longer afford them any amusement, when they put an end to his existence. The signal is then made, and a yoke with four horses is immediately brought in, to which he is fastened and dragged off at full speed. Six officers are appointed to superintend, and see that no unfair advantage is taken and every man who kills a bull is rewarded according to his merit, which they decide. As soon as one was taken away, another is admitted, and the same scene of cruelty was reacted till they had dispatched seventeen, my feelings however would not allow me to stay to the conclusion. To make any farther remarks in this occasion would be needless, reason & humanity loudly declaim, but it is to be hoped that ere long these relics of barbarism will be entirely abolished.

Thus much for the bull fight, I shall now refer to a more pleasing scene, & take a view of the Lima Ladies in a situation more becoming the delicacy of their sex. During our stay here, several balls were set on foot, to which we were always invited, but I shall only mention that at the palace, which was given by the Viceroy on the 28th. The rooms were very long, several appartments having been thrown into one, which were well lighted up with chandeliers. All the first families in Lima were here collected, and afforded a grand display of Spanish beauty, of which I am sorry to say I was much disappointed. There were some pretty but very few handsome women, and they wanted much of that easy air, and grace, which so characterizes our country women.

The Viceroy himself, though by no means a young man, led off with a minuet, several boleros and cotillions followed, after which they commenced the country dances, which continued the whole Evening. The supper was very elegant, but consisted chiefly of ices, which were prepared in different manners, and tastily arranged. After this they danced again for some time and kept it up till about half past three, when they all dispersed.

The ladies of this city have a singular custom of concealing their faces, when they go abroad, by a large hood, which is placed in such a manner, as only to leave a small aperture for the left eye. Whether this is to preserve beauty, or conceal deformity I will not pretend to say. It is however a complete deception, and often produces great mistakes, as age can never be distinguished. The custom of weaving the hair (which is very long) plaited behind, is still in fashion tho' not quite so common as a few years ago when every woman had a tail.

Both sexes are very much addicted to smoking, the pernicious effects of which are very evident, for it is quite a rare thing to see a person with a good set of teeth; the ladies seldom indulge themselves in public, but they are so extremely fond of it, as frequently to get up in the night to regale themselves with the delicious fumes.

The next day we made a party to visit the ruins of Pachacamac, an ancient Peruvian town, about 20 miles to the northward[25] of Lima, near which is a country seat of the Marquis of Montemera, who kindly offered us every accommodation in his power. Although not a little fatigued with our exertions the preceding night, we commenced our journey in the cool of the evening, which in these countries is by far the best time to travel. The road excepting the first three or four miles, lies entirely through a barren sandy desert, which had we crossed at any other time, we should have found most insufferably hot. On one side it is bounded by the sea, which was distant about 4 miles, and on the other by a chain of mountains equally stereil. Such we were told was the general aspect of the country along shore from which it extends ten, twenty, & sometimes thirty leagues. In these desarts however there are several insulated spots, of green where vegetation is luxuriant, and the traveller may be supplied with every refreshment, for this soil is naturally so very productive, that wherever there is water there will be verdure. Here we met several large droves of mules both coming from, & returning to the country, chiefly laden with grain, but always observed that those which returned, brought nothing with them. In this manner all the inland trade is carried on, and it is astonishing with what expedition they travel, and what fatigues they will undergo. The mules in this country are very fine, and, as they have no other means of conveyance, the roads being so extremely bad, are the most useful animals, indeed many of them are used in the carriages at Lima.

On our way, we saw several air plants which are extremely curious, as they have little or no root, and grow loosely on the surface of the sand, where no other vegetable will thrive. Our attention was now turned to a singular phenomenon which we had never before observed, occasioned by the reflected rays of the setting sun on the sand of a distant mountain. The whole summit seemed to glow with fire, and had a most beautiful appearance and it was sometime before we could convince ourselves that it was not snow, which we had seen produce a similar effect at the Peak of Teneriffe. We travelled slowly on account of our horses, as we had some distance to go the next day, it was therefore late before we arrived. The Marquis' house is curiously situated on the top of a steep mount, which completely overlooks his estate, and commands a most extensive view. Here we met with a hearty reception, but as all the party were very much fatigued, we retired early to rest. In the morning, we were much struck with the beauty of our situation which the darkness of the night prevented our observing before. We were in the centre of one of those insulated spots where nature seems to have lavished her choicest gifts. Here were I a poet I should say, that

> Nature casting o'er the direful waste,
> Relenting stop'd, and pitying drop'd
> A tear for human woe, which water'd
> All the plain, and of a desart,
> Made a garden smile

The whole is highly cultivated, and watered by the river Loraine,[26] from which a neighbouring village takes its name. After breakfast we again mounted our horses and set out for Pachacamac which is about four miles distant. We re-crossed the Loraine by a neat stone bridge which was built by order of the former Viceroy, who in many instances, seems to have been very desirous of improving the country. It is of a singular construction, being an inclined plane supported by several arches gradually descending from a steep hill on one side to the valley on the other. From the top of this we had an extensive view of the dreary desert we had so lately passed, and leaving the road a little to the right, soon arrived at the ruins above mentioned. The name Pachacamac (or the place of the Unknown God)[27] was given to this town by way of distinction, in reference no doubt to the temple of the sun, so celebrated by the first conquerors of the country, the remains of which are here still to be seen. The ruins of this place are very extensive, and considering the rude materials with which it is built (mud and unburnt bricks) it is surprising that it has not long since been totally demolished. The climate however is greatly in its favor, and many of the streets and public buildings may still be traced. The former are narrow, but perfectly strait, and cross each other exactly at right angles. The houses have been small but substantially built, and many of them appear to have had an upper story. The doors are very low, but what is most remarkable, we could not discover any windows or other apertures for admitting light. This is a deficiency observable in all the ancient buildings of this country and, as it seldom rains, in any part of

Peru, were probably placed in the roof. To the right on an eminence which over looks the whole town, and the greater part of the adjacent plain, is a wonderful, and prodigious mass of buildings, consisting of a temple dedicated to the Sun, a palace of the Inca, or King, and a fortress, all of which are so nearly connected that it is difficult in their present ruined state to ascertain the appartments alotted to each. They occupy the whole of the summit, which is about a mile in circumference the exterior buildings forming a complete square. It has been surrounded by three complete walls, one above the other. The lower wall or glacis, as I shall term it, is certainly the most surprising, and considering the implements of war then in use, is built according to the first principles of science, and fortification. The declivity of the hill is cut down almost in a perpendicular direction, and faced completely round to a considerable height, with a rampart eight or ten feet in thickness, supported by buttresses at equal distances, which at that period when arts, and arms were in their infancy must have rendered it a place of no inconsiderable strength. These having been the strongest parts of this building, are as may naturally be supposed the most perfect. The rest which is little more than a confused heap of ruins, did not however escape our observation, and we had the satisfaction of beholding the temple of the Sun, which had been the chief object of our research. It is said to have

Portrait of Allen Francis Gardiner.

An earlier victory for Hillyar and the *Phoebe*: the battle of Tamatave, 20 May 1811.

The main target of *Essex*'s depredations: two South Sea whalers (note the whaleboats in davits along the broadside of the nearer ship).

A miniature portrait of
Captain James Hillyar
by an unknown artist.

Captain David Porter
of the United States
Navy

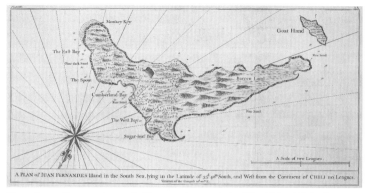

A PLAN of IUAN FERNANDES Illand in the South Sea, lying in the Latitude of 33.d 40.m South, and West from the Continent of CHILI 110 Leagues. Variation of the Compass 10.m 00.m E.

Plate from George Anson's *Voyage Around the World* (published 1748) with his survey of the main Juan Fernandez island.

Pictorial chart of Callao by Luis de Surville, 1778.

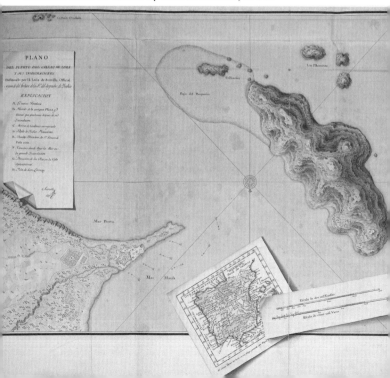

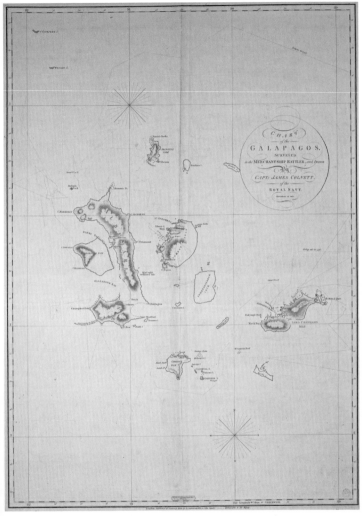

A chart of the Galapagos Islands by Captain James Colnett, 1798.

This watercolour by Captain Edward Fanshawe records the spectacular sunrise over the Andes as his corvette HMS *Daphne* approached Valparaiso in June 1849.

Rounding Cape Horn was not always traumatic. Here recorded in another Fanshawe watercolour, *Daphne* makes the passage under all plain sail.

Essex and her prizes at Nuka Hiva in November 1813.

A view of Valparaiso Bay in the middle of the nineteenth century, by Harry Edgell.

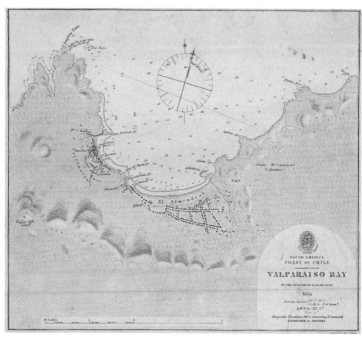

A chart of Valparaiso Bay, as surveyed by the officers of HMS *Beagle* in 1835.

The final stage of the battle: the crippled *Essex* is at centre with *Phoebe* to the left and *Cherub* right.

been very richly ornamented, and in many parts to have been covered with plates of gold and silver. However this might have been, little now remained to render it an object particularly worthy our attention, sufficient however to give us an idea of the state of advancement to which its founder must have arrived in the common arts of architecture. There are several curious specimens of painting in large patches on different parts of the walls they are of a light red, laid on over a smooth surface of plaister with which all the appartments seem to have been lined. At a little distance in the valley is the monastery of the daughters of the Sun, having been a building appropriated for the Inca's daughters, but at present is much decayed, and only frequented by the muleteers in their passage across the desert. Several of the burying places have been opened by the Spaniards, as it has been reported that a great deal of treasure was there deposited when the town was evacuated. How far their expectations have been answered is impossible to say. Some may have succeeded, but to what amount will never be known.

Numbers of human skulls, and bones were scattered about in every direction and with very little trouble we found some of the cloths in which they had been buried. These must have been interred at least 300 years, but what is most astonishing the colors were still remaining. About ¾ of a mile from the town is the grand divisional wall, which runs entirely across the plain, and separates it from a neighbouring district, which was formerly subject to a different government. It is about 12 feet in thickness, built of brick, and perfectly strait. Those parts which are the most perfect are from 18 to 20 feet high, and were probably much higher, which at that time must have been attended with prodigious labour, and expence. Such are the monuments left us by these unfortunate people, untaught by science, and unacquainted with the civilized part of mankind, yet naturally industrious, and strictly adhering to the dictates of reason, they have in some measure surmounted these difficulties, and left a lasting memorial to the confusion of more favored nations. And while contemplating this extensive scene of ruin, and devastation could not help repeating these lines.

* "When Cortez furious legions flew
  O'er ravish'd fields of rich Peru,
  Struck with his bleeding peoples woes,
  Old India's awful genius rose:
  He sat on Andes topmost stone,
  And heard a thousand nations groan;
  For grief his feathery crown he tore
  To see huge Plato foam with gore:
  He broke his arrows, stamp'd the ground

---

*Warton[28]

To view his cities smoking round
What wars he cried hath lust of gold
O'er my poor country widely roll'd!
Plund'rers proceed! My bowels tear
But you shall meet destruction there.
From the deep vaulted mine shall rise
Th'insatiate fiend, pale Avarice:
Whose steps shall trembling justice fly
Peace, Order, Love and Amity!
I see all Europe's children curst
With lucre's universal thirst;
The rage that sweeps my sons away
My baneful gold shall well repay."

Although the site of this town and the surrounding country are considerably above the level of the sea, from which it is at least three miles distant, the surface is in many places covered with muscles, and a variety of other sea shells, which evidently prove that at some period or another, it must have been deluged. This however could not have taken place since the foundation of this town, which was probably about 400 years ago; or considering the materials with which it is built, must have been totally demolished.

The day now becoming very hot, and having rather exceeded our time, we returned to the Marquis', to dinner, much pleased with our excursion. Here we remained till the Evening, when taking leave of our hospitable friend, we returned to Lima where we arrived about 8 o'Clock.

The next day, being the last of the year, we repaired on board, being desirous to attend the ball given on that occasion. After dancing for some time, we learnt that several of our partners were engaged to another in Lima, to which they requested us to accompany them. Such an invitation from a lady was not to be refused, and having previously offered to escort them up, it was accepted with double pleasure, not withstanding our former fatigues. Here we met a very pleasant party, and kept it up till about 5 o'Clock in the morning, having according to custom danced out the old year and danced in the new. After breakfast we took a ride in the country and in the Evening returned on board.

I shall now mention the few particulars which I have been able to collect, respecting the revolution in this country.[29] The native Americans have naturally an implacable enmity to the Spaniards, of whom they are extremely jealous. These, monopolize every place of confidence, or profit, in which great abuses are allowed, and nothing is left for these poor people, but calmly to endure the yoke. This seems to have been the great breach which has been continually widening as civilization increased. The Chilians are a much more industrious, and hardy race of people than their neighbours to the north-ward, here, therefore, it was natural to suppose the spirit of revenge would first break forth.

They declared their independancy about two years ago, since which they have been warmly engaged in its support. The inhabitants of Buenos Ayres, and Rio Plata, who had long been struggling under the Spanish yoke, took advantage of this juncture to strengthen the common cause and raising a body of troops sent them under the command of General Belgrano, to their assistance. Both parties acknowledge Ferdinand but the revolutionists entirely disown the junta of Spain, and its representative the government of Lima. At the beginning of these disturbances, General Guayameche was sent out to take command of the troops in this country where he has been very successful. He has however been lately superceded by General Pezuela, who is now with the army. The American Consul who resides at St Iago[30] has so far ingratiated himself with the opposite party, that they have allowed him a command under their General Carrera. This certainly is a very political measure as his countrymen have always been desirous to insinuate themselves into this part of South America, but if the Peruvians get hold of him, it will most assuredly cost him his neck. The forces were at this time divided, part being in Peru, & part in Chile, at both which stations however the royalists have been frequently beaten. The whole force of the latter amounts to about 10,000 men, but if we may judge of them by the few specimens we have had at this place, they must be bad indeed; ill disciplined, and wretchedly provided. The greater part were collected to the Southward, and we found Lima almost entirely garrisoned by a newly raised militia called the Concordia.

As it is our intention soon to sail for Valparaiso, I will say no more on this subject, as at that place we shall probably obtain a more particular, and authentic account of these proceedings.

I must not however forget to mention our visit to the mines of Casamarquilla la vieja,[31] an ancient Peruvian town, and which, I think much more curious than those of Pachacamac. On the morning of the 8th we set out with a small party for this place, which is about 17 miles from Lima, in a northeasterly direction. We rode for a few miles on the banks of the Rimac, which at this time was so much overflowed as often to oblige us to go out of the way leaving the plain which is tolerably cultivated, the road lay over several steep, and barren mountains which we passed by the most narrow, and rugged paths, where I had no idea that a horse could venture. They are however extremely sure footed, and so accustomed to this kind of travelling, that they will proceed without danger by the brink of the most frightful precipices.

As we proceeded, we observed several remains of ancient fortifications, which certainly have been executed with a great deal of skill, some of the mountains having been almost entirely surrounded by high walls, and all the passes to them completely infiladed. Many of their works may still be traced in different parts of the country, which evidently prove that its former inhabitants must have been a warlike race of people. Descending from the mountains, we again found ourselves in an extensive plain, which was well watered and laid out in fields & pastures. The sun was now rising fast, and it had every appearance of being a hot day. We therefore quickened our pace having determined to satisfy our curiosity before we took any refreshment. About twelve o'Clock we arrived at Casamarquilla, which is situated in the centre of a large sandy plain, about three miles from the foot of the Andes. The ruins of this place are about 4 miles and ¼ in circumference but as they have very much the same appearance as those of Pachacamac I shall not give them a particular description but confine myself to the subterraneous magazines which are really very curious. These are to be met with in almost every part of the town, but particularly in that in which the fortress is supposed to have been built. They are all separate; of considerable depth, and regularly lined with brick, a small aperture only being left, at the top, just sufficient to admit a man. In these granaries a great quantity of provisions have been deposited, particularly corn, as is evident from the number of husks and ears which in many of them are still to be found. *One of our party, out of curiosity, allowed himself to be lowered down into one of them, which was about 12 feet in depth. The surrounding earth, had in some measure fallen in, under which no doubt there was still a quantity of grain, so that it might probably have been much deeper. By merely turning over the surface with his hand, he discovered several ears & husks of Indian corn, some specimens of which, he brought up to our no small satisfaction. These extensive magazines must evidently have been made to provide against a scarcity of provisions occasioned either by famine, or war, from which we may draw the following conclusion, that the ancient inhabitants, at least of this part of Peru, must have been an industrious and warlike people. Without war there could have been no scarcity, for the soil is here so very productive that with the least pains it will afford all the necessaries of life; nor is it reasonable to suppose that a people who could execute a work of this kind with so much ingenuity and judgment should be too indolent to cultivate their own lands. Indeed if we consult the accounts given by the contemporaries of Pizarro they will completely authenticate this supposition. Had it not been for the intestine wars, in which they were at that time engaged, the Spaniards would certainly have met with a considerable resistance, and bought

---

*Mr Cussons

their conquests more dearly. Zarate,[32] in his account of this country, mentions a singular piece of policy in the distribution of their lands, of which half only was allotted to the inhabitants. The remainder was equally divided and disposed of partly to the revenue and partly for the defraying of Religious expences. So that in case of dearth, which seldom happened, one half, which was equally cultivated with the rest, still remained for their subsistence: and, in case of war, were probably laid up in the granaries above mentioned.

This much for antiquities; we will now turn our eyes from the subterranean vaults, and take a view of the stupendous Andes, whose towering heights gradually rise till they are lost in the clouds. Before us lay the mountain road, which leads to a narrow pass at a considerable height by which alone they are accessible, in this part of the country. There are several others, but as this is the nearest, and most direct to Lima, it is generally the most frequented. On the other side of these mountains where there is a contrary current of air, they are subject to frequent and heavy rains, which are not known in this part of Peru, near the coast, and evidently confirms my former opinion relative to the cause of this phenomenon. Having now been rummaging over this place for more than an hour in the heat of the day, we thought it high time to partake of the refreshments with which we had not forgotten to provide ourselves. Accordingly we retired to a neighbouring cottage, and after making a hearty meal, mounted our horses and returned towards Lima, where we arrived about six o'clock in the Evening.

As the mines in this country, for which it has been so famous ever since the conquest, have been so often described and we had not an opportunity of visiting them ourselves, it will be needless to mention the few particulars which we were able to collect, at present however they are nearly at a stand, many of them having been worked to such a depth that the influx of water will not allow them to proceed any farther. Application has been made to Old Spain for a supply of workmen, and the necessary apparatus for erecting steam engines, from which they expect great advantages. Money here is of such little value, that every thing is proportionally dear, but the number of frauds and impositions, practiced upon strangers is almost incredible, and the most respectable shopkeepers may frequently be beaten down to a third of the price they first ask for their goods. The furniture of the houses though the most shabby I have ever seen, is generally mounted with silver; & should this be left but half an hour under the care of the ostler it is ten to one but the greater part is stripped off & replaced with tin or copper in such a manner as scarcely to be perceptible, workmanship is so very exorbitant, and the artificers so independent that plate would be equally expensive as the pure metal, so that the most common utensils are generally made of solid silver.

The horses of this country are generally very fine, and seldom exceed 50 or 60 dollars though when young they may be purchased for much less. Of wild animals there are a great variety, but as they seldom approach the town, or sea coast, we had no opportunity of seeing any of them, excepting the Lama, and Armadillo, which are certainly the most remarkable. These animals are of a slender form, about the size of a deer, but very strong and hardy, inhabiting the cold and mountainous parts of this country, where they are very numerous. The back is arched, the tail short, and the neck and head resembles that of the camel to which they bear an affinity in many other respects, but particularly in their great abstinence from food. They have no teeth in the upper jaw, and the upper lip is cleft like that of a hare. Their wool which is very fine is of a light brown, but gradually becomes lighter towards the under part of the neck, and belly where it is perfectly white. On the back it is intermixed with long hairs, and has a very disagreeable smell. The head is black, the legs are long, and slender with two toes on each foot, armed with long nails like those of the camel. It feeds very sparingly, but what is the most remarkable, never drinks. This at first I could scarcely credit, but as two of them were sent on board as a

present to the Captain, we had sufficient proof of
this extraordinary peculiarity. They are extremely
nimble, & when irritated spit a quantity of saliva
from their mouths, which naturalists tell us is of a
poisonous quality, and will raise the skin, wherever
it touches it, but this we never found to be the case.
They are held in great estimation on account of
their wool which is manufactured into hats, &
clothing, besides which their flesh is reckoned a
great delicacy. I have only described the Lama, the
Armadillo being very little known. The Vecunna,[33]
& Guanaco, being of the same species as the former,
and the distinction scarcely yet defined it is probably
only their size, what I have therefore said of the
Lama, will apply equally.

It was now determined as I have before hinted,
that we should leave this place for the coast of Chili,
which several circumstances conspired to render a
most expedient measure. Provisions there, we
understood, were much cheaper, and better, and salt
meat although not to be procured on any part of the
coast, might be easily cured. This we had often
attempted here, but without success, the climate
being too warm. Besides this, we should probably be
able to obtain some satisfactory account of the *Essex*,
of which we had here been disappointed, and procure
a sufficiency of provisions, either to take us round
Cape Horn, or once more to go in quest of her.
Accordingly the 11th was the day appointed for

sailing, but as I had by this time made several acquaintances, I was determined not to return on board till the last moment. On the 10th I dined at the palace, and in the evening accompanied some of the party to a bull fight, where however, I only remained a short time, merely for the pleasure of seeing the Ladies. This is the third which has taken place since we have been here; as I have described the first I will not wound your feelings with a repetition.

The next day I took my last farewell of Lima, with all its gaieties, and returned on board, where every thing was prepared for sea. We weighed with the land breeze, in company with the *Cherub* and *Indispensable*, Southseaman, and in a few hours were wafted from those golden shores. This is almost the only ship that has escaped the *Essex*, and as she was homeward bound, to insure her farther success, we took her under our convoy. We made a long stretch to the southward and westward, but did not get into the variables till we were in Lat. 34° S. & Long. 98° W. The wind at first came from the northward, but gradually veering round to the westward, in a few days it came again from the S.E.

On the 2nd of February James Hedges died, having been suddenly attacked with a swelling in his leg, which produced a mortification, and in six days occasioned his end. His loss was much lamented by all; his upright character and good disposition, having endeared him to every one on board. On the

5th we passed the island of Juan Fernandez, and on the 8th arrived at Valparaiso Bay, where to our great joy we found the *Essex* & three of her prizes, one of which was armed, laying at anchor. We passed close along side of her, and came too at a little distance, with the small bower, in 16 fathoms water. The next morning she hoisted a white flag at the Fore with this motto, "Free trade and Sailors rights". This we were prepared to answer, and immediately hoisted our ensign on which was the following in large letters "Traitors offend both God and Country – British Sailors best rights". They then gave us three cheers, which we answered playing God save the King, and were in great expectation that they would go out.[34] We proceeded however without delay to complete our water, & obtain the necessary supplies, which was effected by means of the *Emily*'s boats, an English South Seaman, which we found laying here, our own not being allowed to go on shore. Our ensign we soon found had the desired effect, and several of her men deserted, but as she did not seem willing to engage us, we weighed on the 15th: & put to sea determined to keep her under a strict blockade. We did not however find this by any means a pleasant station, for being obliged to keep so near the land we were frequently becalmed and drifted a long way off shore: while, on the other hand, it sometimes blew so strong that it was with great difficulty, by carrying a press of sail, we could keep to windward of the port.

On the 23rd the *Essex* got underweigh, and stood out, probably with an intention of trying her sailing; but we soon obliged her to run into the harbour, and had we been a little farther to windward should certainly have cut off her retreat. On the 25th she set fire to the *Hector*, one of her prizes, which was partly full of oil. In this instance, as in many others they certainly did not respect the neutrality of the port, as she was fired within a cables length of the Frigate, and drifted from one fort to the other, but a short distance from the anchorage.[35] Fortunately the wind was off the shore or the Spaniards would have paid dearly for their temerity. On the 27th they made another attempt, nor could they have had a better opportunity for bringing us to action, singly, which they professed to be their intention, as the *Cherub* was then becalmed a long way to leeward, and could not possibly have come up under an hour and a half.

They both[36] came out with all sail set, the *Essex* having three flags flying, a jack at the Main & the two before mentioned at the Fore & Mizen.[37] We lay too till they were nearly within gunshot, when in the act of wearing round, to give them our starboard broadside, they hauled to the wind and we once more chased them into the bay. Accounts were now received of an English Frigate being on her passage round Cape Horn, which gave us great reason to think they would not remain here much longer, and at the same time made us still more anxious to engage them, before her arrival.[38] Ever since our determination to blockade this harbour we had established signals on shore, of which the Americans were well aware, and on the night of the 27th of March sent a boat out directing her to pull as far as possible to leeward of the harbour, and make the usual night signals at intervals, in order to decoy us from the harbour's mouth, and give them an opportunity of escaping unobserved.

This had so far the desired effect that we mistook it for our own boat, which we had ordered to follow the direction of the enemy, should she come out in the night, and accordingly made all sail after her. We were not however to be duped in this kind of manner, but suspecting the trick from the first, after having taken a sufficient reconnoitre, as the darkness of the night could allow, we hauled to the wind, and in a few hours appeared again off the harbour's mouth, to the great astonishment of the enemy, whom we found with all their small sails loosed and every thing ready for getting under weigh.

Thus again disappointed, and not a little fatigued, we began to deplore our situation and almost despaired of ever getting her from under the neutral flag. But Providence, who had thus far blessed our endeavors with success, now seemed to favor us in a most miraculous manner. The *Essex* had for some time been riding by a cable & anchor belonging to one of her prizes, that she might be in readiness to cut without risking her own, whenever a favorable opportunity should offer. On the 28th she parted in a violent gust of wind, which obliged her to make sail, as all her other anchors were stowed for sea.

We immediately made all sail, which we could in safety carry, but before we came up with her their main topmast went, which baffled all their attempts to regain the anchorage. Thus situated, they came too, with a spring, determined to sell them selves as dearly as possible. We closed them about 20 minutes after 4, and after a severe action of two hours and 20 minutes, in which they certainly did honor to their flag, and fought till it would have been impossible to have retained their ship any longer, they gave up the contest and struck to HM Ship.

What little honor we might have gained by this action will no doubt be detracted, on account of our superiority, but the *Cherub* had only an opportunity of giving her one broadside, as the brisk fire which was kept up between the two Frigates occasioned such light winds, that she dropped to leeward, and not being able to close us again could not render us any farther assistance.

Before our boats could get on board a great number of the prisoners attempted to make their escape, some by swimming, for they were not above ¾ of a mile from the shore, and others in the pinnace, which they launched from off the booms.

The greater part of these people, as we afterwards found, were Englishmen; but few of them reached the shore. The pinnace was picked up by one of our boats, in which were seven men, in the most deplorable condition, two of them wounded, the boat swamped and several of their companions laying dead in her bottom. I shall only mention one more circumstance, which I think worthy of remark, which is, that almost all our countrymen which were serving on board of her, were either killed, or drowned, and many who were wounded, rather than fall into our hands, though unable to walk, crawled to the ports and dropped overboard.[39]

Such was the unhappy end of these miserable fellows, who but a few days before had sent us a most impious and abusive letter, declaiming largely of their liberty, and styling themselves <u>traitors</u>, in which appellation they seemed to glory. Our loss on this occasion was very trifling, and considering the situation in which we lay, for the last hour and ¼, within musket shot of the enemy, almost miraculous: three men only were killed; our First Lieut., Mr. Ingram, mortally: and 6 men slightly wounded.

The slaughter on board the *Essex*, was prodigious, but as so many made their escape, whilst others were drowned in the attempt, it was sometime before we could obtain a probable statement of their losses, which are as follows. 65 killed, 56 wounded, ten of whom are since dead, and 16 drowned. Having got on board the greater part of the prisoners, and repaired her damages for the present, as well as time would permit. The next morning we ran into the harbour, and anchored along side our prize.

Our First Lieut., who had been wounded in the head, and lingering until this time, was now happily released from his pain, and passed we hope into a better world — In the evening his body was conveyed to the Castle, where it was interred with all military honors, attended by the soldiery, and the greater part of the ship's company, whose tears shed a tribute to his memory more gratifying than words can express or the most costly marble have bestowed.*

All the prisoners which only amounted to 93, were sent on board *La Sacramento*, an old Spanish Ship, which was lent us for this purpose. This was an accomodation for both parties, and as all our people were required to repair damages and get the ship in readiness for sea as soon as possible, it was a great burden off our hands. I was sent on board to take charge of the Prisoners where I remained till 26th of April, when they were all put on board of the *Little Essex*, the armed ship before mentioned, which was fitted out as a cartel[40] and sailed the next day.

I was now turned over to the *Essex* which I had

See Note 3rd. Page 161. [page 129 of this edition]

been previously ordered to join. The next day the *Tagus* arrived, which we had been expecting for some weeks; the *Cherub* in consequence was dispatched to the Marquesas Islands, where the *Essex* had left several of her prizes. By this time the *Phoebe* was again ready for sea, and this Ship, although she had been greatly cut up, completely rigged.

Thus much for ships & fighting; we will now change the scene for one more pleasing, and give some description of this place and our excursions on shore.

The Town of Valparaiso is a poor shabby looking place, built without any degree of regularity, excepting the curve of the bay, along which the buildings are continued to a great distance. It is divided into two parishes; that near the landing place, called the port, the other El Mendul;[41] they are both however connected, and each contains a church. The houses are in general built of mud or unburnt bricks, and covered with tiles. The largest do not exceed two stories, and few of their rooms are well proportioned, being frequently many feet broader one way than another.

In the building or appearance of this town there is nothing particularly worthy of remark. The churches are mean, and the Governor's house a shaby looking place. The harbour is defended by three forts; one near the landing place, and the other two at the extremes but they are badly constructed and ill situated, being completely commanded on the land side. The anchorage is good and well sheltered, excepting to the northward, from which point it frequently blows very hard in the months of May, June, & July – violent gusts sometimes come off the land, but as the anchorage is so near the shore have little effect on the sea – In the night it is generally calm. The best births are nearly opposite the Castle about ½ a mile from the shore, where there is from 9 to 10 fathoms & a stiff muddy bottom; moor N.W. & S.E. with a good anchor offshore.

In coming into the bay from the Southward it is necessary to haul close round Point Angelo, which is the Southernmost extreme, otherwise much time will be lost, and you will be obliged to make several tacks before you can fetch the anchorage. Off this point there are several rocks, some of which appear above water. The largest ship may, however, go within ½ a cable of them where there is 15 fathoms water.

The country about the bay is wild, & mountainous, but capable of the highest cultivation: however, such is the indolence of the inhabitants that excepting a few detached spots, there is not a tree or shrub of any kind to be seen for many miles.

About 120 miles from the coast, are the Andes, within which is a range of very high mountains, whose summits are continually covered with snow. These have a most beautiful appearance when the Sun is setting, the reflected rays of which, cover their hoary heads with a mantle of gold. The climate of this country is the most delightful in the world. The sky is generally serene, and they are not subject to those sudden changes from heat to cold which is so often experienced in our own. The soil is in general extremely fertile, & in the interior, I am given to understand, in a tolerable good state of cultivation, and produces all the necessaries of life in the greatest abundance, not only supplying their own wants, but those of Peru, with which, before the war, they carried on an extensive trade in corn, tallow, & hides. Besides this, they grow a great deal of hemp, which is exported to Europe, and considered the finest in the world. Bread, when we were at Lima, had risen, in consequence of the war, to twice its former value. We found it here remarkably good and every thing extremely cheap. Few of the inhabitants of this town are very rich, as the merchants & principal people generally reside at Santiago, the capital of Chili, which is about 90 miles distant. They are however very hospitable to strangers, to whom their houses are always open, & the first salute on entering is invariably "how do you do"? "take a seat." The women are pretty and in general very fine figures. Their beauty however does not last long, for after they are past 30 they begin to decline very fast. It is very extraordinary, that in this, as well as in most other countries, our own excepted, the Ladies are more partial to foreigners than their own countrymen. Whether this is the case with all, I know not, but the English seemed to be in great repute while we were here, and I have frequently known them, at a dance, refuse a Spaniard that they might have an opportunity of dancing with one of us. If curiosity as it has often been said is a part of the female composition, the women here have certainly a large proportion; you cannot be five minutes in their company, although a perfect stranger, but you must give an account of your name, age, business, and friends; and such is their memory, that with the mere mention of your name, they will recall the most trifling circumstances. This however must be attributed to their manner of life, & want of education to afford them less trivial subjects for conversation. Their occupations are but few, and they are kept in such strict confinement by their mothers, without whom they cannot appear in public, or even go abroad.

They have a singular custom here as well as in Peru of drinking Mattee,[42] which is a herb prepared and used in the same manner as tea, for which however it is by no means a good substitute. It is made in a silver cup with a narrow mouth & sipped through a tube about six inches long. This they pass from one to the other as the mohawk does his pipe, without even wiping it, which by the bye is not the most delicate thing in the world. But delicacy here is very little studied at their public & indeed private parties – If you happen to be at all in favor with the Ladies, you will have enough to do to finish the little scraps of cake, and sweetmeats, which they will present you, after they have eaten a part; or to drink their wine after it is honored with their lips; to refuse which, would be considered a great insult or at least extremely rude

Shortly after our action, Captain Hillyar went to Santiago with an intention of negociating between the two contending parties, having been requested by the Viceroy, when at Lima, to exert his interest on his behalf, of which they were both equally desirous.

He was received in the most handsome manner by the Governor, & soldiery, who came out some distance from the city to meet him. Talka, a small town about 800 miles N.W. of Santiago was then the scene of action, & there, after some persuasion, he agreed to go.[43] Both parties seemed anxious for a reconciliation—The Spaniards naturally jealous, & suspicious were fearful lest some other power should take a part in their quarrel & thus in some measure weaken their interest in this part of the world, while the revolutionists, on the other hand, were continually dunn'd with the successes in old Spain, from whence they soon expected their enemies would receive a considerable reinforcement. Thus situated, notwithstanding their various successes, the Limians agreed to sign the treaty & a peace was accordingly concluded, by virtue of which, the ports of Chili, were to enjoy a free trade for the space of one year.

When the news arrived in Valparaiso, the joy and satisfaction seemed to be general: The Royalists who had been confined were liberated & *Viva el re Viva la patria* was echoed in every direction, even by many who had before been adherents to the opposite party. The illiberal policy of the Spaniards had now been put to the test. Ever since the conquest they had endeavored to keep their people in as gross a state of ignorance as possible, that they might feel themselves more dependant upon them. Artificers & mechanics, were everywhere discouraged, and this, added to their natural indolence, has had the desired effect. At this time there was not a man in Chili who could make a musket, nor would it have been possible for them, without the assistance of Europeans, to have carried on the war much longer. True it is they had supplies from Buenos Ayres, but these would soon have been cut off, and their whole plan defeated. This was good policy but founded on bad principles, & certainly reflects little honor to the humanity of the projectors.

About three weeks before the peace was concluded, the Governor of Juan Fernandez arrived with all the people from that island, excepting three men who voluntarily remained behind. Conception had fallen into the hands of the Limians, and it was daily expected they would make an attack upon this place, which, as they were not able to defend it, was thought better to abandon. It will probably be some time before it is settled again, as it was only an expence to the Government, & they find it more advantageous to send the convicts into the interior where they are of great utility in cultivating the lands.

We were now all ready for Sea, the Captn. had returned, & we were only waiting for the dispatches from Buenos Ayres, as it was reported there was another American Frigate in these seas. On the 21st of May however the *Briton* arrived, & relieved us from all anxiety on that account. Both she and the *Tagus* had been sent round in search of the *Essex*, which it was supposed in England had escaped us. Had they come out before all the trade was destroyed, they might have been of some service, but John Bull like, after the horse is stolen he keeps the stable door shut.

On the Evening of the 22nd we had a strong northerly gale, which we had expected for some time. It continued till 25th & brought a heavy sea into the bay. We rode it out very well, two of the Merchantmen parted a cable, but received no other damage. As the *Tagus* & *Britain* [*sic*] were going to Lima & the latter was only waiting for her water; it was determined we should all sail together; the 31st accordingly was the day appointed. On the 30th I went on shore for the last time to take leave of

Valparaiso & all my friends in this part of the world. It was not however, I must confess, without some regret, as it was in all probability the last time that I should ever see them. Such is the natural flow of the affections, that when at a distance from those we love best, we frequently form acquaintances which divert for a time, but often occasion a pang. The next morning we warped out of the harbour, & in the Evening sailed with a sea breeze. As there was a probability of there being an enemies Squadron in these seas, it was proposed we should look into Juan Fernandez before we parted company. We accordingly steered for that island, which we made on the 5th of June, & after reconnoitring Cumberland Bay, where indeed it was scarcely possible for a ship to lay, the wind then blowing fresh from the northward. We parted company with the *Briton*, & *Tagus*, & made sail once more for old England.

From this time we had fresh gales from the northward for several days, which brought us into 45° Latitude & 83°.30 Longitude after which it drew round to the Southward, & Eastward, & became more moderate. In one of these gales above mentioned Manilla Francisco unhappily fell from the Fore top, & received so severe a wound as to occasion his death, in two days afterwards. He was much regretted by all & as we had only sixty effective men on board, not including three wounded Americans, was certainly a great loss to the ship.

On the 17th we had a strong breeze to the North, which took us into the Latitude of the Cape when it suddenly shifted round to the Eastward, & in less their an hour brought us under our stay sails. The weather notwithstanding the wind was off the land, was extremely mild & might be called pleasant, were it not for the frequent fogs, which were often so thick that it was with great difficulty we could keep company with our consort. The gale continued for three days, after which the wind again shifted to the NW. and soon wafted us to the eastward of the Cape which we passed on the 27th in the 58° Latitude.

Nothing could have been more favorable than our passage thus far; which, at this time of the year, we expected would have been attended with some bad, and certainly a considerable deal of cold weather. On the contrary, we had a fine steady breeze, and never found it so cold as I have often felt it in the month of November in England, and nothing to compare to what we first experienced when we came round. The winter is generally considered the best time to return, as the Westerly winds are then more prevalent. This however we did not find to be the case, but they are so very irregular, sometimes blowing alternately in opposite directions, that little dependence can be placed upon them. In coming round from the Eastward it is advisable to make Staten Land, but not to run through the Straits of Le Maire unless the wind is free, as there is such a rapid current that ships have sometimes been rendered unmanageable, & frequently in danger of going on shore. After having made sufficient northing to clear all the land, which will be about 57°, it is better to stand on to 77 or 80 till you turn your head to the northward, that in case of a westerly gale, you may have a good offing from the shore, which is very dangerous, and little known. Returning from the westward, similar precautions must be used, although it would be better not to make Staten Land, excepting with a fair wind.

As the wind was from the NW. we went to the Eastward of the Falkland Islands, where we expected it would come round more to the Southward. Here we were visited by a great number of Port Egmont Hens; so called by Capt'n Cooke on account of their being so numerous at that place.[44] They are of a dark brown color, the belly & under tips of the wing are white. The former however is sometimes of a light brown inclining to red, which is probably a distinction of the sexes. In size and manner of flying they are very similar to the common hen, and little inferior in quality.

On the 14th Evening of July, being a little to the Southward of the river Plate we had a heavy gale from the Eastward which did not however last long, but like that which we experienced nearly in the same latitude on our first arrival in the South Seas, seemed to be the last effort of the troubled elements, after which we had a succession of fine pleasant weather.

On the night of the 27th the *Phoebe* spoke an English brig which informed us of the battle of Toulouse,[45] and the various successes of the allied armies on the continent; in consequence of which a general peace had been declared throughout Europe. From the accounts we had received at Valparaiso by the overland dispatches from Buenos Ayres, we were in some measure prepared for this welcome news; it was not however received with less joy and enthusiasm. Like an electric shock it passed almost instantaneously from one to another, and though we were not in that happy land of plenty, when the inward feelings of the heart break forth into public rejoicings, and festivity, yet it was not less gratifying to observe the secret joy, and chearful countenances of our honest tars; many of whom having devoted their lives to their country, might now return in peace to their homes and families.

A string of events, of such importance, bustling at once upon our view, after having been nearly sixteen months from our native land, and almost out of the way of any communication, gave birth to sensations scarcely to be described, and made us still more anxious for our arrival in Rio Janeiro. On the 26th we made the Land, but the wind failing in the Evening, we were obliged to come too, off the harbour's mouth, and went in the next morning with the Sea breeze.

We had now performed a voyage generally considered tedious, and dangerous, under the most unfavorable circumstances, and with a smaller proportion of men than has ever been known before. Our masts & rigging were greatly damaged, our ship leaky, and our whole crew, officers included, only amounted to seventy; fifteen of whom, from sickness were rendered useless.

Notwithstanding these disadvantages, although we had not a little trouble as may well be supposed, we met with no accident and indeed made better weather than our consort the *Phoebe*, who in the gale, which we experienced off the River Plate, shipped a heavy sea, which washed a boat from her stern, and completely carried away the larboard gangway.

Thank God, we had a most excellent passage, or it would have been worse; our bowsprit was completely decayed, insomuch that in getting it out, which was our first consideration, it broke off by the head. Soon after our arrival we were put in commission, and I had the good fortune to be appointed Second Lieutenant. A hundred and seventy men were sent on board collected from the different ships, & we were all very busy in getting ready for sea, but as we were obliged to make a new bowsprit, there being none in store, we were delayed a considerable time.

On our former arrival at this place from the necessary duties of the expedition, we had few opportunities of visiting the shore, or of forming any just opinion of the country or its inhabitants. We were now almost in the same situation, which altho' it did not preclude my going on shore, prevented me, in a great measure, from making many observations, which I have now only to report. On landing now, I was forcibly struck with the appearance of the place which seemed far to exceed the description, I gave on our first arrival. It was then a mean, and shabby looking place, but was now a large & handsome city. Such is the effect of comparison, by which all our judgments, however erroneous, must be formed – In the former instance we had come from England in the latter from Chili. This difference however may not be without its utility, for by connecting the one by the other, I shall be able to draw a more impartial conclusion.

The churches, which in general first attract the notice of a foreigner, in every, but particularly in a Catholic country, seemed to have lost much of that splendor, which we had before observed; indeed after having so recently seen those of Lima, which are certainly the finest in the world, it must be supposed they would fall in our estimation, & it would be unjust to draw the comparison – Those of St Francisco & Candella (the latter of which is very conspicuous, being higher than any other building in the city) in internal appearance, are by far the finest, but the Princes Chapel, which is also the Cathedral, is certainly neater, and more richly ornamented.

The opera house, which I have not before mentioned, is well situated, forming part of an extensive square, but in point of appearance has nothing very remarkable. It is however extremely neat commodious & well arranged, capable of containing about three thousand spectators. Fronting the stage is a large box appropriated to the Royal family, which is elegantly fitted up, and has certainly a very fine effect.

As to the performance, not being acquainted with the language, it would perhaps be presumption for me to give an opinion, but if I may be allowed to judge from action, & tone (without a judicious management of which, the best written pieces lose their effect), it would be far from flattering to the Portuguese dramatists. The music, and dancing are certainly the best part of the entertainment, but the latter is really carried to such an extreme, that it could not be allowed in a less libertine society, and I am proud to say would be hissed off a British Stage.

Excepting in commercial affairs, the English, who are very numerous in this city, have little intercourse with the inhabitants. Naturally jealous, and suspicious, they keep themselves, but particularly the female part of their families, extremely close; not only from the observation of foreigners, but from their own countrymen, so that, excepting at this place, we had few opportunities of seeing the latter. I was going to say the fair part of the sex – This appellation however the greater part of them do not merit, indeed, as I believe I have had occasion once before to remark with respect to Canada that the influence of Venus never extended to the new world. But perhaps I am too severe – The late emigration from Europe has added many to that number, yet it is universally allowed that the few English females that were resident here outvied them all.

Several Balls were given during our stay (but only one by a Portuguese) all of which we had the honor of attending; the latter was given by the Marquis of Riosacka, a man who had risen from a low birth to his present situation & was now considered the richest man in the Brazils. The rooms were large, and handsome, & extremely well furnished with a degree of elegance, and taste, far exceeding any thing we had reason to expect in this part of the world. The dances no doubt, out of complement to us, were English, and the party extremely agreeable, though there was a less display of beauty than I had expected. The manners & dispositions of the Portuguese are well known, nor do I think it an unjust remark of a traveller, that the inhabitants of Spain and Portugal, have degenerated in their colonies. How is to be wondered at: five sixths of the inhabitants of this country are negroes, & the greater part of the remainder a mercenary set, drawn together by that all powerful magnet, gold.

The females of every civilized country have a certain privilege by which they are at once the umpires of delicacy, and good manners; and such is the natural roughness of unsoftened man that when they are wanting in this respect he is apt to degenerate into the opposite extreme. I do not however mean to intimate that it is entirely the case here, but which I am sorry to say has in some measure induced me to make this remark; yet when we consider the little attention that is paid to their education, & the manner in which they are brought up, surrounded with a tribe of negroes, & servile domestics, from their infancy, whose interest it is to flatter, and peril to refuse, ignorant, and vicious, great allowances must be made.

The interior of this country which is very mountainous I am told is little cultivated, but in general so rich and productive that it is almost entirely covered with wood. Grants of land may easily be procured and when they are in the vicinity of water are certainly very profitable, as the value of the timber will more than repay the expence of clearing them.

In the interior however it is customary, as in the north to set fire to the woods, but much time and labour is required in preparing them for cultivation, which makes it scarcely worth the farmer's trouble. Besides, the well known treasures with which nature has so abundantly supplied the inhabitants of this country from her bowels, coffee, sugar, & tobacco, are the only articles to which they pay much attention, & these indeed require little care, springing up almost spontaneously, ensuring them at once the markets of Europe. The wood of this country is extremely valuable, and well known in England, particularly that from which it derives its name.

By this time we were completely ready for sea, and only waiting for the *Nereus*[46] which arrived on the 1st of Sept. from the river Plate. On 15th we weighed in company with the *Phoebe* and the above mentioned ship, and once more proceeded on our voyage, not a little rejoiced at having our head again turned towards Old England.

After a few days northerly winds, we fell in with the S.E. trades, which we found much fresher, and more to the Southward than we had reason to expect, and crossed the equinoctial on the 3rd of October in 23°.30 Longitude, nearly in the same part at which we had passed it in coming out.

On the night of the 4th being extremely clear I observed the clouds passing each other nearly in opposite directions from the N.E. and S b.E. the former appearing much lighter and higher than the latter – this I think sufficiently proves the hypothesis of a contrary current of air existing in these latitudes occasioned no doubt by those which are constantly rushing in to restore the equilibrium which becoming gradually rarified ascend & return to a denser region.

How far this may be the case, I cannot pretend to say; nor is it probable that the motions of so changeable an element can ever be reduced to any certain rule – The breeze continued with little interruption till we arrived in 5° North when we experienced four days calms and light winds, but attended with little rain, and did not get the N.E. trade till the 10th being then in 9° 30 Lat. & 23° 00 Long. In the afternoon we were struck by a very heavy squall, which although it did not continue more than ten minutes and we had taken the precaution to shorten sail and lower the Topsails, we were in great danger of losing our masts. Fortunately however nothing went, and from what at first appeared, imminent danger, we soon discovered a sensible benefit, the wind having drawn further aft. On the 16th being in Lat. 20° 30 N & Long: about 31° 00 W. we fell in with a French merchantman, bound to the West Indies, a circumstance which I consider particularly worthy of remark, not only from its being the first I had ever met with at sea, but the first time I had seen the White Ensign displayed, which we at first mistook for a Portuguese.[47]

What a wonderful change has taken place in the affairs of Europe, since we left England, the memory of which will ever reflect glory on the British nation and be handed down with enthusiasm to posterity.

We had now a fine breeze from the N.W. and on the 30 fell in with the homeward bound fleet from the Cape and Isle of France, under convoy of the *Danemark*.[48] In the Evening we parted company in great expectations of making an excellent passage, but on the following day the wind veered round to the Eastward and increasing to a heavy gale continued without any intermission for a week.

Our disappointment on this occasion, being then within four days sail of England, can only be conceived by those who have been in a similar situation.

On the 7th of November, however, it became more moderate, but it was not till the 11th that the favoring breeze at length arrived which springing up from the S.W. soon wafted us to our native shores. On the evening of the 13th of November we made the Lizzard, & on the next day anchored in Plymouth Sound.

Finis

Note I

Yes Phoebe twas a piteous sight,
To see thee in so sad a plight,
Without thy quiver, arrow, or bow,
And cover'd with impervious snow.
How changed that eye, which once so bright
Dispel'd the thickest gloom of night
And stooping o'er the briny verge,
With silver tip'd the rippling surge
And dancing all the midnight long,
Awoke the sea boys am'rous song;
But now with ice, incrusted o'er,
Thy tuneful lyre shall sound no more
Thy wintery eye has lost its glance,
Thy stiffen'd feet forget to dance
And hapless lovers shall deplore
And curse, the sad ill fated hour
That led thee from thy wanted plains,
To bear these sad Pa'gonian chains.

Note II

Thoughts occasioned by a distant view of Lima.
Here, have I sat in thoughtful strain
With eyes subverted on the plain,
Nor mountain, shade, or purling stream,
Were wanting, to enchant the scene,
In nature's lap I slumb'ring lay
And Fancy led me far away,
Old Thames has water'd Rimac's shores,

And Oxford, ris'n in yonder tow'rs,
E'en Blenheim too, has found a place
Unworthy such a dastard race,
And Rosamondine bow'rs have shed
Ambrosial fragrance, round my head.
But fonder scenes than these by far
Press on my sight, intrude my ear,
While wafted to my native plains
Where love, & peace, and friendship reigns,
Well have I marked each walk,[1] each seat,[2]
The neighboring hill,[3] the close retreat.[4]
The flow'ry meadows, or the grove,
Where oft my childhood lov'd to rove,
And ev'ry flow'r, and ev'ry spray,
Seem'd to solicit me to stay,
And gently wisper'd in my ear,
Something I would gladly hear,
I've join'd the gambols on the green,
And hug'd the social fire within,
Where conversation blithe, and gay,
Pure as wild, prolongs the day.
My father's well known voice I've heard,
And list'ning dwelt on every word,
And that best, dearest, friend, late giv'n,
By angels wafted up to Heav'n;
But oh! forbear delusive thought,
Forgive my dream, thus dearly bought,

---

[1] Pink walk. [2] Boathouse. [3] Fir Tree Hill, [4] Flower Garden

My Soul could now pour forth in tears,
But now a ray of light appears
And points to yonder heav'n above,
Where Angels dwell, and God is love;
I rise confounded, yet was pleas'd,
And felt my soul unburden'd, eas'd.
And ere I left the cool retreat,
I Carv'd my name upon the seat.

Note III

In Britons cause, he fought, he bled,
And now is number'd with the dead;
And Britons tears bedew his grave.
The last, sad, tribute, of the brave.
No polish'd marble meets the eye,
No blazon'd 'scutcheon flames on high,
Deep graved in ev'ry honest breast,
Far nobler tomb! he long shall rest,
And way worn strangers passing near,
Shall greet the hero, with a tear.

ADDENDUM[49]

Copy of a Letter from Mr. Samuel Thornton Jr. Midshipman on board of H M. Ship *Phoebe*; addressed to his Father, descriptive of the Action between that Ship & the American Frigate *Essex*.

———————————

Late United States Frigate *Essex*
Valparaiso Bay 12th April 1814

My dear Father

Providence, has been pleased to grant success to the *Phoebe* in a comparatively short, but very bloody contest with this ship, after visiting Juan Fernandez, Guyaquil, the Gallipagos Islands & Lima in company with the *Cherub* Sloop War of 18 guns. We had been in search of the *Essex* for the last nine months, during which time she had taken 13 English South Seamen—You may judge of our surprise on rounding the point of the harbor, in finding the object of our search before our eyes, at anchor in the Bay, in company with 3 of her Prizes, & a 20 Gun ship called the *Essex Junior*, which she had fitted out & commissioned as an American Man of War. It is needless to add that immediate preparations were made for Battle on either side, tho Sir James Hillyar never intended to infringe the law of Nations by breaking the neutrality of the Port. In this condition we ran along side of the *Essex*, as she laid at anchor & Sir James hailed her, hoping that Captn. Porter was well (for they are old Friends). He was answered in the affirmative by Captn. Porter, who returned his compliments, but added, If the *Phoebe* touches the *Essex*, (for we were very near) it will be productive of serious consequences. I <u>must</u> act on the defensive. Upon my honor Captn Porter, I do not mean to touch you cried our Captain, I respect the neutrality of the Port, & only came alongside for the purpose of enquiring after your health. His answer was, Excuse me Captn Hillyar in calling my Boarders. Fie, Fie, cried Captn Hillyar, I'm ashamed of you, I thought you Knew me better Sir than to think I would break my word, you have no occasion to be so alarmed. I am not alarmed cried our Yankee Hero, vociferating the words: Stand by my Boys. When in a moment the *Essex*'s sides & rigging, like Scotts' Hill in The Lady of the Lake, were filled with Yankee Warriors true, to the number of 340, armed with Pistols & Cutlasses. The *Phoebe*'s sides exhibited the same warlike appearance on a moment, & thus we backed astern of her, amidst the shouts of the Spaniards on shore, & of the Crew of the *Emily*, an English Ship, that was laying here in durance vile, ever since the *Essex* had been in Port. We then came to an Anchor as close as possible, & the *Cherub* anchored alongside the *Essex Junior*, so close that there was no peace at night for the noise that these Sons of the Lion & Eagle made, & their nocturnal disputes were not unentertaining; Such as, You Rascals we've found you at last, have we – Yes cried the Yankees you have found the worst job you've had to do since you've left England, we will give you *Java*'s time for it &ca.[50] The Yankees then struck up a Song, Let Britain no longer lay claim to the Seas. It was very soon answered by Rule Britannia which the whole crews of the *Cherub* & *Phoebe* both joined in. The next morning at 8 o'Clock, the usual time when Men of War hoist their colors, the *Essex* hoisted a large white flag, Motto, Free Trade & Sailors Rights. This was answered by the *Phoebe*'s hoisting a St George, Motto, God & Country, Sailors best rights, Traitors offend both, (We having been told a number of <u>Englishmen</u> had entered the *Essex*). Under this Ensign the *Phoebe* fought. Upon supposing that we meant to call every man a Traitor on board of the *Essex*, she manned her Rigging, & gave us 3 cheers as a challenge. They were instantly returned by the *Phoebe*, after which our little band struck up God Save the King; during this time our Men stood in the rigging with their Hats off; & a finer sight never was seen, than after the first stanza was played, when we cheered again, & the *Essex* answered our cheers, & struck up the rights of Man. The *Phoebe* completed her Provisions & then went out of the Harbor.

For 7 Weeks we were kept in suspense, when on the Morning of the 28th of March, the *Essex* came out to give us battle. She had scarce got out of the Harbor, when a sudden Gale of Wind carried her main topmast away. She then hoisted three American Flags, & anchored. Captain Hillyar collected his Crew & in a peculiarly impressive manner implored the Divine assistance in their endeavors, after which he addressed them in a short but spirited speech which concluded with these words, Do your duty my Lads, & you can't be afraid. There is no fear of it echoed 300 mouths. God save the King was then given for the watch word and in the case of boarding & at ½ past 3 the action commenced by the *Phoebe*'s crossing the *Essex*'s Stern & discharging her broadside. Our first attack lasted ½ an hour, & upon our retiring, the *Essex* cut her Cable & dropped alongside us, with an intention to board us, which by Captn. Hillyar's superior Seamanship we avoided, & at the same time raking her so severely, that she gave over the idea of closing with us, & maintained a very warm fire for 2 hours more, but from our keeping as far from her as we could, so that her short Guns might not take effect, we both avoided a great portion of her fire, & tore her to pieces with our double shot. She cut our rigging to pieces with her grape, but the heavy firing had occasioned such a calm, that our Sails would have been no use to either of us, so we lay like two logs battering at one another, but fortune always placed the *Phoebe*, (I don't know how) in such a position that we continually raked her, when she having 63 men killed, & upwards of 70 wounded, struck her Ensign, but kept <u>Free Trade</u> &ca flying, her other Flags being shot away. We therefore gave her several more broadsides, before she sent a man to haul this Flag down, but a shot took him Flag & all, just as he was in the act of striking it, & so put an end to the business. The dead silence which immediately ensued was a great contrast to the noise which had just ceased. All the Englishmen on board of the *Essex* now jumped over board, except a few who attempted to save themselves by getting a shore in a Boat, & she swamped under the stern, & they were all drowned. About 40 of those who jumped overboard reached the shore. I was in the first boat that boarded her, nothing was to be seen all over her Decks, but dead, wounded, & dying. We threw 63 overboard, that were dead, & there were several wounded, that it would have been a mercy to do the same to, for the Surgeons only being able to amputate two limbs at a time, these poor creatures were laying about with their limbs shattered, & sometimes quite shot off, weltering in their blood, & no one to assist them. One poor fellow who had his thigh shot off, managed to crawl to a Port, & tumble himself into the water, which put an end to his misery. There were 44 amputations performed that night. Many of the wounded were huzzaing, & the words we fought for, "Liberty", were in all their mouths. Captn. Porter was in tears when he went on board of the *Phoebe* to give up his Sword, & he told Captn. Hillyar 15 of his brave fellows we killed after she struck. Poor Ingram the 1st Lieut of the *Phoebe*, who was with me in the *Amazon*, a tall handsome man, is among the number of killed. All the rest of our officers are well, & not one wounded. Ingram was buried on shore with Military honors. Captn. Porter & the American officers attended. They are now on their Parole on shore, & have liberty of 100 miles, but must be here on the 28th, when we expect to sail for England. The *Essex Junior* has since capitulated—we have taken her Stores out, & she is to bring the Prisoners to England, where she will be considered the *Phoebe*'s Prize. We have done our business very well in the South Seas, & Captn. or as he is now styled Sir James Hillyar, (in anticipation of the Baronetage)* will be the 2nd who has taken an American Frigate.[51] I have a good many Indian Curiosities for C. Shore's Museum, which will be the more acceptable, as they came from the *Essex*, & were no plunder, being given me by the American Chaplain, who was a great friend of mine both before and after the action. They come from the Marquese Islands & Otaheita, where the *Essex* was while we were looking for her on the Coast of Peru. I was rated Midshipman a few days previous to the Action & shall get 50 Gs for it.[52] I hope to be at Portsmouth six weeks after my letter.

Signed/ Saml. Thornton Jr.

Note *Captn. Hillyar was made Companion of the Bath, only.

Appendix: related documents

THIS LETTER IS FROM Charles Sampson, *Phoebe*'s Lieutenant of Marines. Also in his papers is a manuscript copy of the poem reproduced below, which may well be the work of Midshipman Gardiner. (National Museum of the Royal Navy, Portsmouth, ref 1999/9)

H. M. Ship *Phoebe*, Valparaiso Harbour April 2nd 1814.

My Dear Mother,

As there is a Merchant Ship to sail from this place tomorrow I have taken the opportunity of writing to let you know I am well. Before this arrives I suppose you will have heard of the *Phoebe*'s action. We arrived at Valparaiso the 15 of February, where we had the good luck of finding the American Frigate *Essex*, which we have been so long looking for. We have been blockading her in this port untill Monday last; at 4 O'Clock in the afternoon, the Enemy came out and the Action immediately commenced and continued till ten minutes past 6, at which time she struck. By the best account I can get the Enemy went into action with 300 hundred [*sic*] men, out of which 170 were Killed, Wounded and missing when she struck her colours to H. M. Ships *Phoebe* & *Cherub*.

The *Essex* is much larger than the *Phoebe*, she mounts 46 Guns, 40 of which were 32 Pounders. I assure you it was very warm work a long time, she gave us some very heavy broadsides which you may guess by the weight of her shot 32 Pounds, and the *Phoebe*'s were only eighteens. We had 1 Offi[cer] and 3 Seamen Killed, and about 6 or 7 wounded.

I believe I am coming home in the *Essex*, it is expected she will leave this port, for England, in the course of Two Months. Adieu.

your ever dutiful Son

Cha.ˢ Sampson

PS. You must excuse this Scrall [letter torn]
busy work here now, every one in ...
a helping hand in these times.

Lines written to the American Frigate Essex *in answer to some Blasphemous and insulting Letters and Verses*

―――――――――――――――――

(Copy)

The Letters and Songs which you have sent us are so highly infamous, we are at a loss how to answer properly such miserable Blasphemous productions – But as some good men are always found in a Multitude however Bad, to them we hold some esteem: for good men hold no private animosities in a Public cause. It is the Blackguard set only who have such wanton, and unmeaning desires; nor are the following Lines in the least meant to reflect on the good – But fearful more impiety may venture to intrude this Ship, we give the following (tho' with much pain) in hopes to restrain such Blasphemy in future ―――――――

We thought that Piety had been,
Of all the human virtues queen,
By all Mankind admitted:
But you a sad disgraceful band,
Flout human Laws, Divine command,
Contemptable and Wicked.

2

'Tis strange Americans should jeer.
What every Nation else holds dear,
and so delight in Evil;
Morality should be a farce,

Religion too a sad disgrace,
So patronise the Devil.

3

Honour never yet has smil'd,
on you a base degenerate Child,
So void of all good Manners;
Whom Hell alone has led astray,
In wanton pleasures sought to Slay,
and wave your Blood stain'd banners.

4

Go view Marquesa's flowery Sod,
Dispising laws of Man and God,
The monster of the times:
Repentance rears her Snaky Crest,
Strikes fear and horror to the breast,
So overcharged with Crimes.

5

alas; the plain's a purple flood,
By wanton Murders Dye'd in Blood,
Who drunk with Savage pride,
With fire and sword th'unhappy ground,
Thou'st laid with heaps of natives round,
of that unhappy Tribe.

6

With minds in Black oppression fraught,
What Insult have you left unthought,
The Prisoner to deride;
Thin legs and hands in fetters bound,
his Head with Tar and Feathers crown'd,
And made him Slave beside.

7

But this were not enough for you,
To please so bad so base a Crew,
Whose cruelty's no bounds;

You flogg'd them for your scornful sneers,
& as the streaming blood appears,
felt pleasure in his Wounds.

8

Then Fear withheld thy bloody hand,
from murder thou inhuman Band,
The Cowards only stay;
Left them on distant Isles to roam,
helpless unpitied and unknown,
From every friend away.

9

Reflection is the Mirror's claim,
You dare not there behold your Shame,
So conscious are you fallen
So deep in Sin, so far you've gone,
Returning's worse than going on,
so compromise with hell.

10

But when the Day of Battle's come,
The Brave shall stand the cowards run,
Each Standard shall be seen,
The Combat shall be heard on high,
Heaven shall decide the Victory,
And Pity weep the Scene.

11

So oft the Brave and Pious Man,
Weeps o're the carnage ere began,
Claim'd by his country's aid
But Blasphemy shall Sculking lay,
In horrid fear in Wild dismay,
And hang its Impious head.

Notes

Introduction

1. Porter, D, *Journal of a Cruise to the Pacific Ocean by Captain David Porter in the United States Frigate Essex, in the years 1812, 1813, and 1814, Containing descriptions of the Cape de Verde Islands, Coasts of Brazil, Patagonia, Chile and of the Galapagos Islands*, two vols, Bradford and Inskip (Philadelphia 1815).

   The second edition 'to which is now added an introduction, in which the charges contained in the *Quarterly Review*, of the first edition of this Journal and examined' was published by Wiley and Halstead (New York 1822).

2. Thornton's letter, included as an Addendum in Gardiner's manuscript journal.

3. For Parker see: Lambert, A D, *Admirals: The Naval Commanders who made Britain Great*, Faber (London 2008), Chapter 6.

4. For the wider war see: Lambert, A D, *The Challenge: Britain versus America in the Naval War of 1812*, Faber (London 2012).

5. Coletta, P E (ed), *American Secretaries of the Navy: Vol.1 1775-1913*, Naval Institute Press (Annapolis 1980), pp101-13.

6. James Horburgh, Hydrographer to the East India Company, to the Chairs of the East India Company 11 Nov 1812: Melville Papers, William L Clements Library, University of Michigan.

7. Haeger, J D, *John Jacob Astor: Business and Finance in the Early Republic*, Wayne State University (Detroit 1991).

8. Herring, G C, *From Colony to Superpower: U.S. Foreign Relations since 1776*, Oxford University Press (New York 2008), p111.

9. Admiralty to Hillyar 1 Mar 1813: Adm 3/260, National Archives, Kew.

10. Lt William Finch USN to Navy Secretary Jones 13 Feb 1813: Dudley, W (ed), *The Naval War of 1812: A Documentary History*, Vol II, US Naval Historical Center (Washington 1992), pp684-5. For a modern assessment of the voyage see: Brodine, C E, 'The Pacific Cruise of the Frigate *Essex*' in Brodine, C E, Crawford, M J & Hughes, C F (eds), *Against All Odds: U.S. Sailors in the War of 1812*. US Naval Historical Center (Washington 2004) at pp1-26.

11. This ship, the *Elizabeth*, was burned at Rio, being insufficiently seaworthy for a passage to the United States. Dudley II, p690.

12. Lynch, J, *The Spanish-American Revolutions, 1808-1826*, W W Norton (New York 1973) examines each country in the region. Chapters 4 and 5 deal with Chile and Peru.

13. Stackpole, E A, *Whales and Destiny: The Rivalry between America, France, and Britain for Control of the Southern Whale Fishery, 1785-1825*, University of Massachusetts Press (Amherst 1972), p76.

14. These activities were already familiar to the crew of HMS *Phoebe* when she reached Valparaiso. They form the subject of the fourth verse of the bantering poem sent over to annoy the Americans. See Appendix.

15. Crawford, M J (ed), *The Naval War of 1812: A Documentary History,* Vol III, US Naval Historical Center (Washington 2002), pp772-80 reproduces the key correspondence. Greg Dening's chapter 'The Face of Battle: Valparaiso 1814.' in *Performances*, University of Chicago Press (Chicago1996), pp79-98 offers a Pacific islander perspective, but renaming Captain Hillyar as Hillyer suggests other aspects of the story were of less interest.

16. Dixon to Admiralty 30 Apr & 6 Sep 1813, Heywood to Dixon 10 May 1813 rec'd by Dixon 3 Jun 1813: Graham, G S & Humphreys, R A (eds), *The Navy and South America, 1807-1823: Correspondence of the Commanders-in-Chief on the South American Station*, Navy Records Society (London 1962), pp89-91.

17. Dixon to Admiralty 11 Jun 1813, and Admiralty minute of 6 Aug 1813: Graham, pp92-3.

18. Dixon to Hillyar secret 1 Jul 1813 & 5 Jul 1813: Graham, pp99-101.

19. Manley Dixon to Hillyar secret Rio 1 Jul 1813: Hillyar MSS, National Maritime Museum AGC/23/7 & Dudley II, pp713-4.

20. Dudley II, p711.

2. Commander William Black, HMS *Racoon* to the Admiralty 15 Dec 1813: Dudley II, p714; Graham p149.

22. Long, D, *Nothing Too Daring: A Biography of Commodore David Porter 1783-1843*, Naval Institute Press (Annapolis 1970), p146.

23. Hillyar to Admiralty 28 Feb 1814: Graham, pp129-33.

24. Porter to Downes 10 Jan 1814: Crawford III, p708, suggests using the second ship was 'a contingency Porter seems not to have anticipated'.

25. Porter to Navy Secretary Jones 13 Jul 1814; Crawford III pp.715-6; the ex post facto nature of the claim raises doubts, while the

failure of all those on the *Phoebe* to mention the matter suggests Porter may not have recalled the events precisely.

26. Log Book of HMS *Phoebe* 8 & 9 Feb 1814: Adm 51/2675, f151, Crawford III, p712. For a sample from the war of verse that occupied the attention of the officers and men during the long stand off see Appendix.

27. Dening, p87.

28. There is no conclusive evidence of Gardiner's authorship, but the verses were found in the papers of Charles Sampson, the *Phoebe*'s Lieutenant of Marines at the time of the battle. Another poem, similar in tone and vocabulary, from 'A Midshipman of *Phoebe* to the Crew of *Essex*' is known to have been delivered to the American ship: Crawford III, p722 gives the text.

29. Thornton's letter.

30. Ingram was much loved, and Gardiner reports his funeral ashore; Thornton noted his height.

31. Boatswain's Report: Crawford III, p741.

32. Thornton's letter.

33. Dening, p92.

34. Porter to Navy Secretary Jones 3 Jul 1814: Crawford III, pp730-39.

35. Hillyar to Admiralty 30 Mar 1814 & 26 Jun 1814: Adm 1/1950, nos 264 & 300. Log Book of HMS *Phoebe* 28 Mar 1814: Adm 51/2675, ff173-4. Log Book of the *Essex* 28 Mar 1814, as published in the *New York Evening Post* 8 Jul 1814: Crawford III, pp719-730.

36. Letter of 2 Apr 1814. See Appendix.

37. Graham, pp141-97.

38. Log of *Phoebe*, a small format volume, probably Hillyar's personal copy, well bound, with coastal views and charts, including Valparaiso, covering the period March 1813 to October 1814: MS87/026, National Maritime Museum.

39. Dixon to Admiralty 10 Jun 1814, enclosing Hillyar to Admiralty 30 Mar 1814: Graham, pp141-2.

40. Dixon to Admiralty 5 Jul 1814, enclosing Hillyar to Admiralty 11 May 1814: Graham, pp145-6.

41. Dixon to Admiralty 8 Sep 1814, enclosing Hillyar to Tucker 14 Apr 1814: Graham, pp147-8

42. Winfield, R, *British Warships in the Age of Sail. 1793-1817: Design, Construction, Careers and Fates*, Seaforth Publishing (Barnsley 2005), p166.

43. Long, pp160-1. Dening, pp88-9.

44. Farragut, D G, *Reminiscences*: Crawford III, pp757-9.

45. Crawford III, pp760-68.

46. Porter, *Journal of a Cruise*, 1815 ed: Crawford III, pp708-9.

47. Porter *Journal of a Cruise*, 1822 ed.

48. Crawford III, p709 admits the claims were excessive, but accepts the premise that the diversion worked.

49. Dudley II, p296. Long, p162.

50. Long, p159 citing *The Times, Naval Chronicle, The Annual Register* and *Marshall's Naval Biography.*

51. For a discussion of Barrow's role in promoting and publishing naval scientific expeditions see: Lambert, A D, *Franklin: Tragic Hero of Polar Navigation*, Faber (London 2009).

52. Gough, B M, *The Royal Navy and the Northwest Coast of North America 1810-1914, a study of British Maritime Ascendancy*, University of British Columbia (Vancouver 1971), pp15-17.

53. Log of HMS *Phoebe* 11-19 Sep 1813: Adm 51/2675.

54. File of coastal views of South American islands. Includes views of Juan Fernandez and Mas Afuera from Byron's voyage, *Phoebe, Tagus*, and *Beagle*. Adm 344/2255.

55. Shilibeer, J, *A Narrative of the Briton's Voyage to Pitcairn's Island*, printed for the author by J W Marriott (Taunton 1817), pp152-4.

56. Shilibeer, pp155-8.

57. O'Byrne, W, *Naval Biographical Dictionary* (London 1849), pp387-8.

58. Boase, G C, revised by Matthew, H G C, 'Gardiner, Allen Francis', *Oxford Dictionary of National Biography*, Oxford University Press (Oxford 2004), entry 10353, accessed 5 Nov 2012.

59. O'Byrne, *Naval Biographical Dictionary*, p1178.

60. See Lambert, *The Challenge*, pp402-48 for the post-war cultural construction of a new American identity.

The Journal

1. An armed storeship belonging to the North West Company. A Letter of Marque allowed its bearer to act as a privateer: that is, a privately owned warship, legally entitled to act against its country's enemies.

2. Actually *La Miquelonnaise*, an 18-gun privateer. *Unicorn* and *Stag* were 32-gun British frigates.

3. In classical mythology Atlas was a Titan forced to bear the weight of the heavens on his shoulders; in some versions of the myth he was transformed into the Atlas mountains in North Africa.

4. The outward-bound East Indies trade convoy escorted by the British frigates *Doris* and *Salsette* (the correct form of her name)

and the Sixth Rate *Porcupine*.

5. The attack on Santa Cruz de Tenerife on 24 July 1797 was beaten off with heavy casualties, including Nelson himself, whose right arm was so badly wounded it had to be amputated.

6. East Indiamen of 567 and 604 tons respectively, they were both built in 1802 and were making their last round-voyage to Bengal, their fifth and sixth respectively for the East India Company.

7. 'Crossing the Line' was traditionally celebrated with rough horseplay visited on those who had never previously crossed the Equator by seamen dressed as Neptune and his attendants. It often featured dowsing in unpleasant concoctions and mock shaving with blunt instruments. Officers escaped this indignity by paying a forfeit, usually something alcoholic.

8. From *The Seasons*, the best known work of the Scottish poet James Thomson (1700-1748), who also wrote the lyrics for 'Rule, Britannia'. The second line should read 'Where, undisguised ....'

9. From *The Task* by William Cowper (1731-1800).

10. *Cherub* and *Racoon* (the correct spelling) were of the same design, both ship-rigged sloops rated at 18 guns but actually mounting 26, the main battery comprising powerful but short-ranged 32pdr carronades, of the type that also formed the main battery of USS *Essex*.

11. Now Isla de los Estados, Argentina.

12. Properly, Más a Tierra, meaning 'Closer to Land'; this Chilean territory is now known as Isla Robinson Crusoe.

13. The Napoleonic usurpation of the Spanish throne in 1808 had destabilized Spain's South American colonies, which encouraged independence movements and factional infighting. Britain was an ally of the legitimate government in Spain but attempted to remain neutral in the South American conflicts, so Royal Navy officers on station needed to act with diplomatic caution.

14. At this period the word 'crazy' suggested flawed, cracked or in poor condition; it is spelt 'crazzy' in the manuscript.

15. During his epic expedition against the Spanish in 1740-1744 which included the capture of the famous Manila Galleon and concluded with a complete circumnavigation of the globe.

16. A Scottish sailor from William Dampier's privateering expedition marooned on the island in October 1704. He was rescued in February 1709 by another privateer, Woodes Rogers, whose account of his voyage included details of Selkirk's ordeal and inspired Daniel Defoe's fictional *Robinson Crusoe*.

17. Ships in the South Seas whaling trade.

18. Zoologically speaking, these would be caimans not alligators and

iguanas, which are certainly much prized as food but are not a species of alligator.

19. This well-known couplet is from a hymn by William Cowper (1731-1800); as a sailor, Gardiner might well have quoted the less familiar lines that follow:

> He plants His footsteps in the sea
> And rides upon the storm.

20. A hugely successful poem published in 1742 by Edward Young (1681-1765). Gardiner is not quite word-perfect, but it is given here as he wrote it.

21. Albemarle is now known as Isabela island and Narborough as Fernandina.

22. Now Santiago.

23. The British designation for a type of stand-alone gun tower, usually supporting one or two cannon on pivoting mounts on top. Large numbers of them were built along England's south coast during the Napoleonic Wars as anti-invasion defences, so whenever the British saw similar structures they referred to them as Martello Towers.

24. Refers to Ambrose Bernard O'Higgins, 1st Marquis of Osorno (c1720-1801), rather than his more famous son Bernardo (1778-1842), the celebrated leader of the fight for Chilean independence. Ambrose was born in Ireland but chose to serve a Catholic monarch as a colonial administrator, rising to become Viceroy of Peru from 1796 to 1801.

25. It is actually to the south.

26. Now the Lurín.

27. Actually from Pacha Kamaq, the creator god of the Ichma people who inhabited the area before the Inca invasion in the fifteenth century.

28. Joseph Warton (1722-1800), 'The Revenge of America'. Later versions have the historically accurate Pizarro rather than Cortez in the first line; 'huge Plato' refers to the Rio Plata, the River Plate.

29. At the time of *Phoebe*'s visit south America was in the early stages of what would become a long drawn out, complicated and bloody series of wars culminating in the establishment of independent states in the ex-Spanish colonial provinces. The Spanish king, Ferdinand, had effectively been deposed in 1808 but the Spanish had reacted to the French invasion by setting up regional juntas (councils) and eventually a supreme junta, which claimed to be the legitimate government. Reaction to the Napoleonic usurpation of the Spanish throne in 1808 varied across south America, but broadly speaking Peru was the centre of loyalist support for

metropolitan Spain, and sought to put down the insurgencies and independence movements emanating from the surrounding provinces.

Britain's position was difficult: on the one hand Spain was an ally, and Wellington's army was actively engaged against French forces in the Iberian Peninsula; on the other, there was considerable sympathy in some political quarters for the aspirations of Spain's colonies. As ever, Britain's real concern was the protection of her substantial commercial interests in South America, best served by peace and stability, and at this time the Royal Navy was instructed to follow a policy of studied neutrality.

For the United States it was simpler. As a country which had recently thrown off colonial rule, it naturally supported the struggle for independence among what it hoped would become fellow idealistic republics – and it hoped to benefit commercially from the political goodwill it would generate in so doing.

For an entertaining general account of the wars of independence see Robert Harvey, *Liberators: Latin America's Struggle for Independence 1810-30* (London 2000).

30. Santiago, Chile.
31. Cajamarquilla.
32. Agustin de Zárate, *Historia del descubrimiento y conquista del Peru* [*The discovery and conquest of Peru*], Anwerp 1555. The first English translation was published in 1581.
33. Vicuña.
34. By internationally accepted convention, belligerents were prohibited from carrying out acts of war in neutral ports.
35. While there was no agreed concept of 'territorial waters', national jurisdiction was widely regarded as 'within cannon shot' of the shore (*ie* waters that could be defended): hence the reference to how close to the forts the prize was burned.
36. The *Essex* was accompanied by one of the captured British whalers, the *Atlantic*, that had been armed and renamed *Essex Junior*.

The relative size and force of the two frigates has been frequently mis-stated, both then and since, but the following is a comparison based on the standard British system of measurement and therefore consistent:

HMS *Phoebe*, 142ft 9in x 38ft 3in, 926 tons. Guns: nominally 36, but carrying 26 x 18pdr long guns on gundeck, 14 x 32pdr carronades, 4 x 9pdr long guns on forecastle and quarterdeck (unofficially, two small carronades – an 18pdr and a 12pdr – were placed in broadside ports).

USS *Essex*, 138ft 7in x 37ft 3½in, 867 tons. Guns: nominally 32, but carrying 24 x 32pdr carronades, 3 x 12pdr long guns on gundeck; 16 x 32pdr carronades, 3 x 12pdr long guns on spar deck.

37. Gardiner has only mentioned one previously, but the other bore the slogan 'God Our Country and Liberty. Tyrants Offend Them'.

38. This ship, HMS *Tagus*, arrived two weeks after the final battle. Another frigate, HMS *Briton* arrived in May.

39. The implication is that they were deserters from the Royal Navy, which dealt so severely with the crime that death was preferable.

40. Cartels were licensed transports for the repatriation of prisoners of war. The were provided with documentation that would allow them, for example, to pass through any blockade.

41. El Almendral.

42. Often spelt maté in English, mate is an infusion of yerba mate leaves in hot water, traditionally drunk out of a shared calbash gourd with a silver rim as Gardiner describes.

43. Talca is actually about 160 miles south of Santiago. It here that Hillyar mediated the Treaty of Lircay (named after a river on the outskirts of the town) between the royalist forces of the viceroy of Peru (whom Gardiner calls Limians) and the Chilean provisional government.

44. Port Egmont in the Falkland Islands. They are actually a species of large skua (*Catharacta skua antarctica*).

45. Fought on 10 April 1814. Having crossed from Spain into France, Wellington's Anglo-Portuguese army and its Spanish allies was held up by a stout defence of Toulouse. By the time the allies entered the city on the 12th, Napoleon had formally abdicated.

46. A British frigate carrying a large amount of specie. Such valuable cargoes were normally transported by warships and in this case it was an added precaution for the three ships to sail together.

47. Gardiner first went to sea in 1810 by which time French commerce had long since been driven from the seas, so this may be no exaggeration. The White Ensign he refers to is the flag of the restored Bourbon monarchy, reintroduced in 1814 and surviving until definitively replaced by the *tricolore* in 1830.

48. Isle de France, modern Mauritius, was captured from the French in 1810. *Danemark* was an ex-Danish 74-gun ship captured at Copenhagen in 1807.

49. This is copied into the back of the journal in the same handwriting as the rest.

50. A reference to the capture of HMS *Java* by USS *Constitution* on 29 December 1812. *Java* was ex-French, and by an odd quirk of fate

had been captured in a squadron action by *Phoebe* and consorts in
1811.

51. The first was Sir Philip Broke, whose *Shannon* captured the USS
Chesapeake on 1 June 1813. Broke was made a baronet, so it was
a reasonable assumption that Hillyar would be similarly awarded.
However, Broke's honour reflected the brilliance of an engagement
in which the Americans held the balance of advantage, whereas
Hillyar's achievement, although faultless, could not be so
considered.

52. His share of the Prize Money, scaled out according to rank among
officers and men for captured enemy ships. For a midshipman, his
estimate of 50 Guineas represented more than two years' wages.

Bibliography

THE FOLLOWING IS A selection of the most relevant further reading, but additional works on specific aspects of the story may be found in the Notes.

For Gardiner's life a contemporary account is John W Marsh, *A Memoir Of Allen F Gardiner, Commander, RN*, James Nisbet & Co, 2nd Edition (London 1857), and there is an entry in William O'Byrne, *Naval Biographical Dictionary*, John Murray (London 1849). A recent equivalent is 'Gardiner, Allen Francis', the entry by G C Boase, revised by H G C Matthew in *The Oxford Dictionary of National Biography*, Oxford University Press (Oxford 2004).

Sir James Hillyar also has an entry in *The Oxford Dictionary Of National Biography*, but the most accessible modern summary of his life is in Nicholas Tracy, *Who's Who in Nelson's Navy*, Chatham Publishing (London 2006).

David Porter is the subject of a modern biography by David F Long, *Nothing Too Daring*, Naval Institute Press (Annapolis 1970), which largely supersedes that by Archibald Turnbull, *Commodore David Porter, 1780-1843*, The Century Co (New York And London 1929). There is also a more intimate portrait by his son, himself a prominent US Navy officer: David Dixon Porter, *Memoir of Commodore David Porter of the USN*, J Munsell (Albany, NY 1875).

Porter's own *Journal of a Cruise to the Pacific Ocean by Captain David Porter in the United States Frigate Essex, in the years 1812, 1813, and 1814, Containing descriptions of the Cape de Verde Islands, Coasts of Brazil, Patagonia, Chile and of the Galapagos Islands*, was originally published in two vols by Bradford and Inskip (Philadelphia 1815), but was heavily revised with numerous cuts and some additional material by Wiley and Halsted (New York 1822). Of the many more recent reprints the best prepared is the edition by R D Madison in the 'Classics of Naval Literature' series, Naval Institute Press (Annapolis 1986), which includes material from both the original editions and explains the publishing history.

For ready access to primary sources, many of the most significant documents, from both the British and American sides, are reproduced in *The Naval War of 1812: A Documentary History*, a series published by the Naval Historical Center, Washington, DC. The most relevant are *Volume II: 1813* edited by William S Dudley (1992) and *Volume III: 1814-1815* edited by Michael J Crawford (2002). There is also a useful annotated bibliography compiled by John C Fredriksen, *War of 1812 Eyewitness Accounts*, Greenwood Press (Westport and London 1997).

Although the naval aspects of the War of 1812 have always attracted a lot of attention in the United States – its successes at sea have been described as one of the 'foundation myths' of the US Navy, rather like the Armada for the Royal Navy – there has not been much published about the Pacific campaign. One of the few books is Irving Werstein, *The Cruise of the Essex: An Incident from the War of 1812*, Macrae Smith (Philadelphia 1969), but a more academic reassessment is C E Brodine, 'The Pacific Cruise of the Frigate *Essex*' in C E Brodine, M J Crawford, & C F Hughes (eds), *Against All Odds: US Sailors in the War of 1812*, US Naval Historical Center (Washington 2004). There is no book devoted to the *Phoebe*'s mission, but the best modern account of its significance is contained in Andrew Lambert, *The Challenge: Britain against the United States in the Naval War of 1812*, Faber (London 2012).

Picking up on the exotic milieu of the operations, and the theatrical nature of Porter's own account, it perhaps unsurprising that a number of novels have been based on the

Pacific voyage of the *Essex*. The earliest was Frank Sheridan, *The Cruise of the Essex or Making the Stars and Stripes Respected*, David Mckay (Philadelphia 1898), and later John Jennings, *The Salem Frigate, A Novel*, Doubleday (Garden City, NY 1946). It also inspired one of Patrick O'Brian's great Aubrey–Maturin novels, *The Far Side of the World*, Collins (London 1984), in which the frigate is renamed USS *Norfolk*. This in turn forms the core of the plot in Peter Weir's 2003 movie *Master & Commander: The Far Side of the World*, although in order not to alienate American sympathies the US frigate becomes a French privateer, albeit an American-built ship.